PAUL

SOLDIER OF PEACE

PAUL

SOLDIER OF PEACE

KENNETH SCHENCK

This book compliments of
Wesleyan Publishing House
P.O. Box 50434 • Indianapolis, IN 46250-0434
Donald D. Cady, General Publisher
Call: 1-800-4WESLEY (493-7539) • Fax: 1-800-788-3535
E-mail: wph@wesleyan.org • Online: www.wesleyan.org/wph

wesleyan
publishing
house

Indianapolis, Indiana

Copyright © 2011 by Kenneth Schenck
Published by Wesleyan Publishing House
Indianapolis, Indiana 46250
Printed in the United States of America
ISBN: 978-0-89827-440-0

Library of Congress Cataloging-in-Publication Data

Schenck, Kenneth, 1966-
  Paul : soldier of peace / Kenneth Schenck.
    p. cm.
  Includes bibliographical references.
  ISBN 978-0-89827-440-0
  1. Bible. N.T. Romans--Textbooks. I. Title.
  BS2665.55.S54 2011
  225.9'2--dc22
                                                    2011013216

To N. T. Wright and Richard Hays

CONTENTS

PREFACE

The first volume of this series, *Paul—Messenger of Grace*, was dedicated to Krister Stendahl and Jimmy Dunn, two pillars of the revolution in the study of Paul that has taken place these last few decades. The key to this revolution was the renewed interest of reading Paul more carefully against his Jewish context. Stendahl's article, "Paul and the Introspective Conscience of the West," was groundbreaking in this regard.[1] His comments in this short piece were so simple and yet so obvious when you return to key texts like Philippians 3 and Romans 7.

And his insights fit very well with the Wesleyan tradition of which I am a part, even though he was a Lutheran bishop. For example, Stendahl pointed out that Romans 7 is not about Paul's unending struggle with sin. Rather, Paul saw the Christian as set free from the power of sin. We will set out this clear reading of Paul in chapter 5. The weight of modern scholarship thus fits well with the Wesleyan tradition at this point.

Nevertheless, it was E. P. Sanders who broke the dam of unexamined interpretations of Paul in 1977 with his benchmark work, *Paul and Palestinian Judaism*.[2] His basic point was that the Jews understood their keeping of the Law as a response to God's grace rather than a way to earn God's favor. Somehow it seems appropriate that Sanders comes from a Methodist background, for other traditions have long accused us of teaching "works righteousness" simply because we believe God expects faithfulness in response to his grace. Once again, the weight of modern scholarship on this topic thus fits well with the Wesleyan-Arminian tradition.

Jimmy Dunn, my own doctor-father, moved the ball along even further, particularly in his study of phrases like "works of law" in Galatians and Romans.[3] He has convincingly argued that Paul's discussion of faith versus works was not some abstract debate over earning salvation but that "works of law" for Paul primarily had to do with those aspects of the Jewish Law that separated Jew from Gentile, things like circumcision, food laws, and Sabbath observance. It was he who popularized the phrase a "new perspective on Paul," and the previous volume was fittingly dedicated in part to him.

I dedicate this volume to two other key figures in the study of Paul and especially the study of Romans: N. T. Wright and Richard Hays. Along with Sanders and Dunn, Wright is generally considered the third in the triumvirate of the new perspective. Although I have not followed him at every point, he has given further clarity to Paul's expectation that works will follow justification. Although I differ a little from Wright on the certainty that all who are initially justified will have the appropriate works to be finally justified at the judgment, I have deeply resonated with his honesty in reading passages like Romans 2:5–10 and 2 Corinthians 5:10.[4] Once again, the direction of modern scholarship fits well with Wesleyan theology.

Finally, this volume is also dedicated to Richard Hays. If Dunn has properly located the phrase "works of Law" as something more concrete than good deeds in general, Hays has argued that Paul could think of faith in terms of *Jesus'* faith and not only our faith.[5] Again, although I have not followed Hays at every point, at one point of my scholarly pilgrimage, I found myself coming to agree with him on at least two key passages in Paul: Romans 3:22 and Galatians 2:16.

I thus dedicate this second volume to Wright and Hays as—along with Dunn and Stendahl—the most important scholarly voices in my own pilgrimage in Romans. Let me also commend Robert Jewett's new commentary on Romans as the best scholarly resource now available. Although it will be demanding for someone who does not know Greek, it encapsulates most of the insights I just mentioned.

What started out as a second and final volume in this series has become the second of a three volume series. This is appropriate because the book of Romans is worth an entire volume in itself. Many thanks to those at Wesleyan Publishing House who recommended and implemented this suggestion. A third volume, *Paul—Prisoner of Hope,* will thus follow, covering the later writings of the Pauline corpus. This volume works through Romans, largely in the order of Romans itself.

The same thanks of the first volume are in order for the second. Thank you to Wesleyan Publishing House for the opportunity to write books of this sort, as well as the Bible studies that are companion pieces. I also blogged through this volume, and I remain appreciative to those who dialoged with me over its ideas.

I continue to thank my family for their tolerance of my constant writing. Thanks to my youngest children, Tom and Sophie, for pulling me away to play catch and shuttle them to soccer and Taekwondo. Thanks to my wife, Angie, and to Stacy for their patience, especially when they wanted to borrow the lap top. And as for Stefanie, she has Paul to thank for the Mac she took to college this year. Thanks to God for the great family he was given me!

March 21, 2010

1

DEAR ROMANS

CLOSING A CHAPTER

Paul had never been to Rome. He had often wanted to go there (Rom. 1:13), but he had been very busy for at least a decade starting and establishing churches all around Greece and what we now call Turkey. Then at the end of what is now known as his third missionary journey, he wrote his best-known and arguably most magnificent letter to Rome. The year was perhaps as late as A.D. 58.

Paul probably wrote Romans from Corinth in southern Greece. In the last chapter, Paul commended a woman named Phoebe. This woman was a deacon of the Eastern port city of Corinth, a place called Cenchrea (16:1). So most scholars agree that Paul was in Corinth when he wrote Romans.[1]

By the time he wrote Romans, Paul had confessed Jesus as his master for about twenty-five years. Before he believed, he persecuted some early Christians. He was a Pharisee and put special emphasis on keeping the Jewish Law along with a large number of strict interpretations of it. He may have thought that God's anger toward Israel was intensified by Jewish Christians just as he thought it was intensified by those who disregarded the Pharisees' rules on how to stay pure. Since Paul worked for some of the leaders of Israel, he had the political power to cause problems for Jewish Christians.[2]

But sometime around the year A.D. 33, the risen Jesus appeared to Paul, who made a complete turnaround. The man who had strongly insisted on maintaining the boundaries between Jew and Gentile became a man who saw in Christ the breaking down of such barriers. Almost immediately, Paul found himself in trouble because of his preaching. Within three years (around A.D. 36), he had to escape the city of Damascus by going down a wall in a basket to avoid arrest (2 Cor. 11:32–33). Soon after, he cut short a visit to Jerusalem because some were trying to kill him (Acts 9:29–30).

Little is known of what Paul was doing during the next ten years of his life. The books of Acts and Galatians indicate he went back to his home country, Cilicia, a region on the southeast side of modern-day Turkey. Eventually, he was drawn to Antioch, one of the centers of Christian activity at the time, second only to Jerusalem. It was from Antioch in the northernmost part of Syria that Paul launched the missionary journeys recorded in Acts.

Paul's so-called first missionary journey (there likely were others that were not recorded) took him and a coworker named Barnabas to the island of Cyprus. Then they went north to the south-central part of Turkey (or Asia Minor, as it was known at the time). Many evangelicals believe that Paul wrote Galatians just after this trip, though I disagree. His second recorded journey, in the early 50s, took him to Greece for the first time. He spent about two years in and around the city of Corinth. On this trip, Paul wrote 1 Thessalonians, which many scholars think was his first surviving letter. He may also have written 2 Thessalonians at this time.[3]

In the mid-50s, Paul spent about three years around the city of Ephesus, during his third recorded missionary journey. It was from there that he wrote 1 Corinthians and two other letters to Corinth that apparently did not survive. Although many disagree, I think Paul's stay at Ephesus ended with an imprisonment that is not recorded in Acts (see 2 Cor. 1:8) and that he wrote Galatians and Philippians during this period as well. When he was finally able to leave the city, Paul wrote 2 Corinthians on his way around the northernmost part of Greece and back to Corinth.

Paul—Messenger of Grace, the first volume of this set, ended right there, with Paul on his way to visit Corinth again.[4] He first went to Corinth around A.D. 50–52. Paul also alluded to a second visit that was not recorded in Acts (2 Cor. 13:1). Then he prepared for a third visit. On this trip, which may have been his final one, Paul planned to take up an offering for the less fortunate among the believers in Jerusalem (2 Cor. 8–9). It was also on this third trip to Corinth that Paul wrote Romans, the fullest expression of his thinking.

Paul's comment in Romans 15:23 describes his thoughts about his situation as he wrote Romans: "There is no more place for me to work in these regions." Paul was still having conflict with the Corinthian church (2 Cor. 10–13). Earlier, he had sent them a harsh letter from Ephesus, one so harsh perhaps that neither Paul nor the Corinthians preserved it. When he wrote 2 Corinthians, Paul was unsure of what he would find when he reached the city (12:21). It seems that no one from Corinth joined the group that accompanied Paul on his journey to Jerusalem with the offering he had raised for the poor (Acts 20:4).

Paul decided not to return to Ephesus on this final trip; instead he invited the elders to meet him at Miletus (20:16–17). The writer of Acts said that Paul was in a hurry. But if Paul's previous visit to Ephesus ended in imprisonment (his brush with death mentioned in 2 Cor. 1:8 and Phil. 1:20–25 may have referred to this time), then he had good reason to bypass the city. Paul's words in Romans, "There is no more place for me to work in these regions" (15:23), seems full of pathos. He was unable to return to Ephesus and the region around it. He had an uneasy presence at Corinth. Certainly he had many opponents in Jerusalem (see Acts 21:20–22) and perhaps even still at Antioch (see Gal. 2:11–13).

Paul's letter to the Romans was written as one chapter of his mission was closing and another beginning to open. Paul was a church planter, not a long-term pastor (Rom. 15:20–21). He did not feel called to preach to Jews, but to non-Jews or Gentiles (see Gal. 2:7–8; Rom. 15:16–18). The door had closed for Paul in Asia Minor and Greece. So he began to look west to Rome and then Spain.

LOOKING TO SPAIN

If we only had the book of Acts for information about Paul's life, we would probably conclude that his mission to non-Jews was the result of being continually rejected by Jews. We might think he targeted Jews and Gentiles equally but was better received by the Gentiles. However, Paul did not view his ministry in this way. He was delighted when Jews believed that Jesus was their promised King, their Messiah. But Paul's primary calling and mission was to bring the good news to non-Jews. He was the apostle to the Gentiles, just as Peter was the apostle to the Jews (Gal. 2:8; Rom. 15:8–12, 16, 18).[5]

Paul also saw himself as a traveling minister rather than being called to a permanent location. He intentionally avoided preaching the good news where someone else had already laid a Christian foundation (Rom. 15:20–21). Perhaps Paul's life verse, which he quoted from Isaiah 52:15, could have been: "Those who have never been told of him shall see, and those who have never heard of him shall understand" (Rom. 15:20 NRSV).[6]

Paul was a church planter. He did not intend to stay in Rome for a lengthy time the way he had at Corinth or Ephesus or perhaps first at Tarsus. Instead, it seems he wanted to set up a mission base in Rome so that he could launch into the un-evangelized territory of Spain (Rom. 15:24).

Paul wrote Romans from Corinth on his way to Jerusalem at the end of his third missionary journey to introduce himself to the already existing group of believers at Rome. He went to Jerusalem before Pentecost (Acts 20:16) with a large delegation from the various churches he had planted (20:4). Together, they brought a large offering for the needy among the Christians of Jerusalem (Rom. 15:25–27; see also Gal. 2:10).[7]

Paul was deeply interested in the Roman churches. He had often wanted to go to them but had consistently been hindered from making such a trip (Rom. 1:13). He hoped that by his visit they could share some mutual building up of each other's faith (1:11–12). He wanted to "preach the gospel" to them, a good thing in itself (1:15).

But Paul's ultimate destination was Spain. Rome was an important stop along the way, and Paul was looking forward to impacting the churches at Rome, but it was not his primary focus. He wanted to get to Spain, and Rome was a fitting place to minister on his way there. Paul might have also expected the churches at Rome to contribute to his mission to Spain just as the Philippians supported some of his earlier efforts.

The book of Romans was thus a letter of introduction to the churches in Rome, which he planned to visit on his way to Spain. While introducing himself, Paul hoped to accomplish at least two other tasks. One was to provide an explanation and defense. Paul had enemies in the early church, and they were talking about him (Acts 21:21). Romans was a systematic defense of Paul's understanding of the gospel and especially, the question of how Gentiles could be saved without converting to Judaism.

The second task was corrective. Rome apparently had groups of stronger and weaker Christians, like Corinth. So Paul took time, while introducing himself and defending his presentation of the gospel, to address disunity among the churches of Rome.

PAUL'S DETRACTORS

Paul was apparently not popular with many of the believers in Jerusalem. When he arrived with his offering for poor believers, James and the elders took him aside to strategize about dealing with his opposition (Acts 21:17–26).

James and the elders informed Paul that most believers in Jerusalem had conservative views on the law. They were upset about rumors they'd heard that Paul was teaching Jews to abandon the law of Moses and not to circumcise their children or follow other key Jewish practices (21:21). To counter this unfavorable impression, the elders urged Paul to participate with other men in a vow they had taken and even to pay for the others' expense related to the vow. The goal was for everyone to see that Paul kept the Jewish Law, despite the exceptions James had made earlier for Gentile believers.

In Romans, Paul confirmed that false rumors had circulated about him. Some had apparently summed up his teaching as, "Let us do evil that good may result" (Rom. 3:8). This slogan was probably their version of Paul's teaching that faith, not works of law, makes us right with God. So Paul explained that he did not condone sin, much less think that it enhanced God's grace (Rom. 6–8). At the same time, he did not consider disregarding certain parts of the Jewish Law, such as circumcision and matters of ritual purity, to be sin.

By the time he arrived in Jerusalem, perhaps some time around A.D. 58, Paul had been sparring with this "denomination" of Christians for quite some time. The author of Acts was more charitable than Paul toward this group. Paul called them "false brothers" (see Gal. 2:4), but the writer of Acts treated them as believers (see Acts 15:5; 21:20).

About ten years earlier, Paul had presented his teaching on Gentiles to Peter, James, and John. He did this privately, because he knew how controversial his teaching would be: a number of Jewish believers taught that you could only be saved if you fully converted to Judaism (Gal. 2:1–10). Though James preferred that Gentiles convert, he did not force them (Gal. 2:12), and this seems to have been the official position of the Jerusalem church (Acts 15).

But not long after this meeting, Paul had a disagreement with Peter at Antioch over Jewish and Gentile believers eating together, an argument he seems to have lost (Gal. 2:11–14).[8] Despite his allowances for Gentiles, James had sent messengers to Antioch to make sure the Jews were still keeping purity rules. Paul disagreed with this action. He believed the purity rules were interfering with the unity of the church. Paul advocated instead that Jewish Christians lay aside these aspects of the Law when they prevented fellowship with Gentile believers. Since Paul did not say in Galatians that his opponents at Antioch conceded his point, it is likely they did not.

This argument probably contributed to the break-up of Paul and Barnabas as a ministry team, even though Acts only mentions an argument about Mark (15:36–40). So as Paul embarked with Silas on his second missionary journey, he was somewhat on the outs with the churches of Jerusalem and Antioch.

James and the Jerusalem elders determined that Jewish and Gentile believers could eat together provided three conditions were met: (1) the Gentile believers did not bring meat that had been offered to another god; (2) they did not kill the meat by strangling, so that the blood stayed in the meat; and (3) they did not participate in sexual immorality (Acts 15:23–29). It seems Paul ignored these instructions, except the part about sexually immorality. Paul's approach to the issue of meat sacrificed to idols was "don't ask, don't tell." Don't ask where the meat came from, and eat it with thanksgiving (1 Cor. 10:23–30).

Paul's first draft of a response to his detractors who also insisted Gentile believers must be circumcised was the book of Galatians. Although some date it very early, I believe Paul wrote it at Ephesus on his third missionary journey. In it, he explained the purpose of the Jewish Law and how a person can be in right standing with God. I personally think Paul wrote Philippians at Ephesus as well, just a little bit later. In Philippians 3, Paul warned the Philippians to be on the lookout for his opponents, "those mutilators of the flesh" (3:2), meaning those who insist Gentiles must be circumcised.

The book of Romans was a later, more developed version of the same material. By the time Paul wrote this letter, he knew his opponents and their arguments well. He knew what others were saying about him, and he had been working on his response for years. He knew from experience what had and had not worked with his response in Galatians. Romans was thus Paul's fullest, most mature defense of the gospel message he preached among the Gentiles. It was not written as a compendium of Christian theology; it was a letter written in a certain context to address a specific situation. But Paul wrote it as an introduction to what he believed and taught, and in that respect, it is the most systematic presentation of his theology on these particular issues.

The church at Rome included both Jewish and Gentile believers. However, the bulk of Paul's rhetoric in the letter addressed Gentiles. Paul said, for example, that he wanted to have some fruit among them just as "among the other Gentiles" (Rom. 1:13). He said he felt responsible for both the Greek and barbarian—a way of dividing the Gentile world (1:14). Later, he explicitly addressed the Gentiles and warned them not to get cocky about God's favor toward them (11:13–14). Even when Paul did speak to Jews, he seemed to be speculating what Jews would say rather than directly addressing the reader (2:17). So while Paul surely expected some Jewish believers would read Romans, he primarily addressed Gentile believers, in keeping with his sense of the mission to which God had called him.

So Romans was a general defense of the gospel Paul preached among the Gentiles, paying particular attention to the objections and arguments his detractors had used against him, especially those in Jerusalem and Antioch. He explained that all have sinned, both Jew and Gentile, and that both thus equally rely on God's grace to be accepted by him (Rom. 1–4). He explained that Christ's obedience had undone the sin of Adam for everyone, both Jew and Gentile (Rom. 5). He addressed the purpose of the Jewish Law and the accusation that he condoned sin (Rom. 6–8). And, he described God's plan and how Jews and Gentiles fit into it (Rom. 9–11).

To a significant degree, the question of how Gentiles could be saved dominated the letter to the Roman church. How could Gentiles be part of the people of God without converting to Judaism? The book of Romans was not an abstract theology of how to get saved, as Augustine and others have led us to believe. When Paul talked about the law, he was not referring to some abstract moral law, but to a specific part of the Jewish Law. When Paul talked about works, he was thinking of the parts of the Jewish Law that most separated Jews and Gentiles. The book of Romans was thus Paul's most developed response to his detractors.

LIFE REFLECTIONS

For several years, I have heard great pathos in Romans 15:23, where Paul mentioned in passing that he had no more room to minister in the eastern Mediterranean. We like to think of Paul as a great, hero missionary who experienced success in every area. But when Paul wrote this verse, it must have seemed like things could go either way. The hindsight of history is often clearer. Our experience of things in the moment often is far from clear.

It is amazing that Paul never gave up. Despite setbacks, he kept moving forward. Sometimes he had to move on the hard way. The Romans forced Paul to move on from Ephesus. He left Corinth without having everyone on his side.

We can draw some relevant truths from Paul's fortunes. First, we will never win everyone over to our sense of God's will and plan, no matter how hard we try or how eloquently we argue. Dale Carnegie once put it in this way, "A man convinced against his will is of the same opinion still."[9] The second truth is that there is a time to move on. It can be as simple as agreeing to disagree or as hard as wiping the dust off your feet. But there is a time to give up and move on.

Sometimes we think the early church was completely unified. The book of Acts contributes to this perception because part of its purpose was apparently to show that early Christians were not troublemakers, but were peaceful and harmonious. And indeed, this is how we are supposed to be. The ideal presented in Acts is God's word for us to emulate. But it is not and was not always the case, even in the early church. The early church had factions too, with distinct ideologies that were as different from each other as some denominations differ from each other today.

On some points, Paul and his opponents genuinely disagreed. His opponents taught what they believed in their communities, and Paul taught his understanding in his communities. On other points, his opponents seemed to have skewed his position to suit their goal of discrediting him. Perhaps they thought they understood him. Perhaps they intentionally skewed his thinking. It is sometimes hard to tell the difference.

While we hope always to agree to disagree and remain brothers and sisters in Christ, our disagreements can easily devolve into calling each other "false brothers" as well. Paul and Barnabas wisely went their separate ways and surely wished Godspeed to each other.

When others maligned Paul with malicious intentions, he did his best to protect his assemblies from their influence. Early on at Antioch, he seems to have argued with them face to face (Gal. 2:11–14). But at some point, he must have concluded that trying to convince them was a waste of time. He got to the Galatians only after they were already partially persuaded. He wrote the Philippians before his opponents arrived (Phil. 3:2–3, 17–19). And most of Romans was a defense of his understanding of the gospel to prepare the way for his anticipated arrival.

There is a point where we have to leave all such things in God's hands. It is, after all, not about winning an argument or everyone seeing that we are right. God can take care of such things. If we are right, God will make this clear in the end. If we are not, God will make it clear in the end as well.

FOR FURTHER REFLECTION

1. For years the assumption in ministry has been if you are faithful, your church will grow in numbers. How accurate do you think this idea is? Can you think of places Paul went in Acts where he did not leave significant churches behind? Does it make any difference to realize that Paul's churches may only have been forty to fifty people in size?

2. Paul was clever, perhaps even inspired, in the way he used circumstances to move forward in his mission. What do you think is the proper mixture between God's leading and human cleverness in moving toward our goals?

3. Paul seems to have attracted enemies in many places—even in the church. Do you think this opposition was all Satan's work or can we learn from mistakes Paul might have made? Do you think the strengths of his personality were accompanied by weaknesses? Why or why not?

4. Philip Melanchthon, who worked closely with Martin Luther, once called Romans a "compendium of systematic theology."[10] Many theologians have tried to make Romans into a system of absolute, ideological truth. But if Romans addressed a situation in the life of Paul and the Roman church—if it is a letter rather than a textbook—how does this fact change how we read it? Keep this question in mind as you move through the next five chapters.

2

IN THE HANDS
OF AN ANGRY GOD?

WHAT MADE PAUL TICK

When someone is upset, you can't always tell from the person's arguments and words what has him or her charged up—the primary, underlying issues. The person may not even realize that the source of anxiety is buried below the surface. To communicate effectively and deal with the actual problem, you may have to dig a little deeper to understand the person's real concern. If, instead, you respond on a purely logical level engaging the person's words and not the underlying issues, you may fail to understand and address the real problem.

In a similar vein, in order to understand the solution Paul offered in the book of Romans, we need to understand what he saw as the underlying problem. E. P. Sanders suggested that Paul's understanding of the gospel actually developed from solution to problem.[1] When Paul experienced the risen Christ, he believed that Jesus was the Messiah. This in turn led him to see Christ's death and resurrection as God's doing. Before this point, Paul probably did not see any problem with the Jewish Law, but if Christ was God's solution, then there must have been a problem with the law. If Jesus was God's way to be right with God, then the Jewish Law was not the way. And if the cross was the way, then Gentiles could be in right standing with God just as easily as Jews could.

We do not have to accept all of Sanders' teaching to benefit from it and see how Paul might have come to his understanding of the gospel. Paul had kept the Jewish Law brilliantly as a Pharisee. If anyone was right with God through the law, then surely Paul was. But then Paul witnessed the risen Jesus and discovered that his law-keeping was insufficient and that it was not the way God had chosen to provide redemption. Rather, the cross of Jesus was God's way of reconciling Israel to himself. Sanders put it rather bluntly: "this is what Paul finds wrong in Judaism: it is not Christianity."[2] Paul did not come to his understanding of the gospel by wrestling with the human problem of sin; his gospel originated with God's revelation to him of the solution in Christ. The Holy Spirit then helped Paul reason back from the solution in Christ to the general problem of human sin.[3]

As a Pharisee, Paul had been taught that one of the primary purposes of the Jewish Law was to serve as a fence, guarding the Jews against defilement from the nations; the cross would have even more radical implications for Paul the apostle.[4] Jesus' agenda for Paul's ministry included welcoming the discarded people of Israel; God revealed to Paul that the inclusion must go further than Israel. If the cross trumped the law as the way to reconciliation and right standing with God, then Gentiles, too, could be included. Some passages must have taken on new meaning for Paul, like Isaiah 11, which he took as a prophecy that Gentiles would believe in the Messiah (see Rom. 15:12).

So Paul, reasoning from the solution to the problem, realized that Gentiles could be right with God through the cross and resurrection of Jesus and that the Jewish Law could not make you right with God. Paul's arguments in Romans and Galatians explain and defend these fundamental understandings.

Jews already acknowledged that they relied on God's grace for a right standing with him.[5] This idea would not have been controversial in any way. They even agreed with Paul that everyone in Israel had sinned and that Israel's good standing with God was a matter of his grace. But non-believing Jews rejected the death of Jesus as a sacrifice to atone for the sins of Israel. And the believing Jews in Jerusalem rejected the idea that Jewish believers were no longer obligated to keep the whole Jewish Law. These underlying positions are the basis for Paul's arguments in the book of Romans.

THE RIGHTEOUSNESS OF GOD

The key verses of Romans are: "I'm not ashamed of the gospel: it is God's own power for salvation to all who have faith in God, to the Jew first and also to the Greek. God's righteousness is being revealed in the gospel, from faithfulness for faith, as it is written, *The righteous person will live by faith*" (1:16–17 CEB). This highly compact statement encapsulates the key ideas Paul argued in the first four chapters of Romans. It establishes key words and phrases, like *gospel*, *salvation*, *faith*, and *God's righteousness*.

Paul started the letter with the assertion that God had set him apart as an apostle commissioned to spread the gospel (1:1–2). The gospel, or good news, was that God had enthroned Jesus as the Messiah, the Promised King. God appointed him "the Son of God with power" (1:4 NASB) by raising him from the dead. The "good news" included everything that went with Jesus becoming king—including salvation.[6]

In Paul's understanding, the phrase *Son of God* meant that Jesus was God's appointed king of the universe.[7] When God raised Jesus from the dead and seated him at his right hand in the highest heaven (see Acts 13:30–34), God enthroned him as "the Son of God with power" (Rom. 1:4 NASB) on the throne of the universe. This is kingship language, meaning that God delegated to Jesus the task of judging and ruling the nations.

The term *salvation* referred to being saved in the coming judgment of God. We often say we are saved from our sins, but this expression is shorthand for being saved from the consequences of our sins. When Paul and other New Testament authors talked about salvation, they were primarily referring to escaping God's wrath on judgment day, also called the day of the Lord.[8]

The meanings of the word *faith* (*pistis*) and its verb form, *believe* (*pisteuō*), range from trust to faithfulness and belief. While these English words (*trust, faithfulness*, and *belief*) each have a distinct meaning, they are nuances of a single Greek word, *pistis*. When Paul talked about the "faith of God" (Rom. 3:3 KJV), he meant the faithfulness of God. When Paul talked about a Christian's faith, his meaning varied from belief that God raised Jesus from the dead (4:24) to a full confidence and trust in the fact that Jesus is Lord (10:9).

But perhaps the most confusion has resulted from Paul's use of the phrase, "the righteousness of God" (1:17 KJV). Paul said that God's righteousness was revealed in the gospel about Jesus the king. From this expression alone, we can trace the birth of Protestantism out of Roman Catholicism and some of the later disagreements among Protestants.

"RIGHTEOUSNESS FROM GOD"

Up until the 1500s, almost everyone in the Western world defined themselves as Christian, and the only church in the West that existed was the Roman Catholic Church.[9] Enter a German monk named Martin Luther. In 1517, Luther publically questioned some of the contemporary practices of the church. That moment in history was preceded, however, by some personal breakthroughs that Luther experienced. One of Luther's breakthroughs had to do with his understanding of Romans 1:17 and the phrase, "the righteousness of God" (KJV). At that time, the vast uneducated majority of Christians did not hear the Bible read in their own languages. Latin was the language of both the scholar and the church, and the Catholic Church read the Scriptures in Latin. In Latin, the phrase "the righteousness of God" is *iustitia Dei*. The first word looks a lot like the English word *justice*.

And "justice" is exactly how the Church understood the meaning of the word: the gospel revealed the justice of God. This is one possible meaning of the word for righteousness (*dikaiosynē*).[10] And it is true that God is just. But most interpreters prior to Luther thought the verse meant that God distributed his justice both to believer and non-believer. Luther, who had a heightened sense of his own moral imperfection, found this verse troubling. At the time, he believed in purgatory, a place where Christians burn off their remaining sinfulness and imperfection after death. Understandably, the justice of God did not seem like good news to him.

Luther's moment of insight was the realization that the phrase "the righteousness of God" (Rom. 1:17 KJV) could also be understood as "a righteousness from God," that is, as a reference to God declaring a person righteous. Thus Luther's theology of justification was born; for him, justification was the act of God declaring us righteous or innocent in his divine court. Luther believed we could never be acceptable to God based on our goodness or morality. We come to God as sinners, and we remain sinners even after we come to Christ. One of Luther's best-known statements is that we are "at the same time righteous and a sinner, as long as we are always repenting."[11]

MIXED REVIEW FOR LUTHER'S INTERPRETATION

Some of Luther's thinking on this point seemed to accurately reflect Paul, while other parts did not. For example, you will not find in any of Paul's letters an expectation or justification for sinning as a Christian (see, for example, Rom. 6:1–2, 12, 15). Romans 7 is often interpreted to mean that Christians are unable to stop sinning. As we will see later, this understanding is quite mistaken. Paul's position on this issue is not even close to ambiguous. He expects Christians to live righteous lives and believes that those who do not are in danger of missing out on salvation in the end.

However, Luther was probably correct in the way he understood Paul's teaching about how a person becomes right with God in the first place. Paul taught that a person is justified (becomes right with God) on the basis of faith or trust in what God did through Jesus Christ, the king (Rom. 3:28). For Paul, such faith was primarily centered on God the Father and what he had done through Jesus. However, since God accomplished these things by raising Jesus from the dead and establishing him as Lord of the cosmos, Paul also spoke of our faith being directed toward Jesus, as well as God the Father.

Unfortunately, it is not obvious in English that the word meaning "to justify" (*dikaioō*) is closely related to the word for *righteousness* (*dikaiosynē*). To justify is thus "to declare righteous." Luther rightly understood this word to be a legal term.[12] God pronounces us not guilty; he declares us innocent in the divine court; he justifies us.

So Luther was right regarding the moment of our initial faith in what God has done through Christ. However, the real trial—the moment of God's assessment that counts—is at the judgment. Paul told the believers at Corinth that they "all must appear before Christ in court so that each person can be paid back for the things that were done while in the body, whether they were good or bad" (2 Cor. 5:10 CEB). He also told the believers at Rome that on the day of wrath, when God's righteous judgment is revealed, God will pay each person according to the works they have done (Rom. 2:5–6). Though Luther is surely right that we are first justified with God on the basis of our faith, Luther failed to see that we will not be finally justified if our actions thereafter do not conform to God's righteous expectation.[13]

Most scholars today also recognize that while Luther's sense of initial justification was mostly an accurate reflection of Paul's theology, Luther was probably wrong in his understanding of the phrase "the righteousness of God" (KJV) in Romans 1:17. The Roman Catholic Church took it to mean the justice God distributed toward believer and non-believer. Luther took it to be legal fiction—God considering us righteous even though we are not.

DEMONSTRATION OF GOD'S RIGHTEOUSNESS

The Jewish background to the phrase points in another direction. Psalm 98:2 is remarkably similar to the verse in Romans: "The LORD has made his salvation known and revealed his righteousness to the nations."[14] Like Romans 1:17, the verse mentions God's righteousness and speaks of it being revealed. It also talks of this revelation going out to all the nations, just as Paul understood the gospel to be for the Gentiles as well as Jews.[15] The verse does not speak of Israel becoming righteous, but of God's righteousness being demonstrated as he brings about the salvation of Israel.

There are other places where God's righteousness and his salvation are mentioned parallel to one another.[16] Isaiah 40–66 is permeated by these sorts of parallels between God's righteousness and the salvation he is bringing. These chapters were of great significance to the earliest Christians, and Paul himself occasionally alluded to them (see Rom. 15:21). The Greek version of Isaiah 51:5, which Paul used, says, "My righteousness draws near quickly, my salvation will come out like a light. The Gentiles will hope on my right arm" (my translation).

With the consistent use of these phrases together in the Old Testament—not to mention in the Jewish literature of the first century[17]—Paul almost certainly inherited the understanding that the expression, "the righteousness of God," referred to God's righteousness as his propensity to save Israel. Paul could certainly have extended or expanded the meaning, but it seems clear his starting point was that God's righteousness was demonstrated by saving Israel. So when Paul said that "in the gospel a righteousness from God is revealed" (Rom. 1:17), he was talking about God's relationship with his people and especially his propensity to save them—God's saving righteousness.

The Greek word translated *righteousness* or *justice* (*dikaiosynē*) was a relational term in Jewish thought. It was not an abstract quality of God but the way God related to his people and the world. It sometimes referred to God's judgment, as we will see in Romans 1:18, where Paul talked about the wrath of God toward ungodliness. But as in Romans 1:17, it could also refer to the good news of how God acted through Christ to bring salvation to his people, including not only believing Jews, but believing Gentiles as well.

So Paul connected with the Jews' existing understanding about the righteousness of God: God's faithfulness to Israel both in judgment and salvation. Then, he extended the idea of God's righteousness to include the work of Christ to bring God's righteousness to Jewish and Gentile believers alike.

It seems that later in Romans, Paul developed the phrase even further, playing on the ambiguity of the phrase, "the righteousness of God."

Perhaps he wanted the audience to hear the meaning Luther later heard. It could be that Romans 3:21 alluded not only to God's righteousness but also to the righteousness God declares us to have. When Paul said, "Now apart from Law the righteousness of God has been manifested" (3:21 NASB), maybe he intended the Romans to hear a dual meaning. Not only has God's righteousness been revealed in a new way through Christ, but also a righteousness is now available for us "of God" or "from God." At least it is possible that Paul had this in mind.

LIFE REFLECTIONS

The standard Protestant application of Paul's theology in Romans goes something like: No one can earn God's favor. No matter how much good you do, it is not enough. Good deeds cannot make you right with God or get you to heaven. You can only get right with God by faith—by believing in Jesus, believing that Jesus rose from the dead and confessing him as Lord.

Most of this summary is consistent with Paul's writings. True, it is removed from the context of Paul's original message, where his key point was whether Gentiles, like the Jews, could escape God's wrath and become a part of God's people. It lacks the original flavor of the debate over works of law, a debate that focused on regulations that separated Jew and Gentile, like circumcision and purity rules. Paul also never said that heaven is our eternal destination, and I will argue later that Paul believed a transformed earth would be our eternal home. And Paul never mentioned hell in his writings.

Churchgoers are usually quite comfortable with the traditional Protestant understanding of Paul's basic line of thought: Every person has done wrong at some point, with the result that God's judgment stands over and against us. Jesus absorbed God's anger toward our sin. All we need to do is trust in what God has done for us through Jesus, and we will escape the coming judgment and be saved. God's provision of a way out for us is an indication of just how loving and righteous he is.

At the same time, I suspect some aspects of this line of thinking no longer make sense to many Westerners in our broader culture, including some Christians. Certainly this does not necessarily mean it is incorrect. Every culture has its blind spots, and we cannot assume that our common sense is always going to be the true sense. Nevertheless, God revealed the biblical messages to their original audiences in ways they could understand. So we have to consider the culture of the biblical authors not only when looking at their ethics (what they said about how to live), but also when looking at their ideas and beliefs.

For example, what exactly does the picture of an angry God mean to say? Anger is a human emotion that usually has an edge of being out of control and, as we now know, actually impairs our ability to think clearly on a physiological level.[18] We can wonder whether a God who is omniscient—and thus for whom there is no difference between experiential knowledge and cognitive knowledge—could literally experience anger.[19] Anger is a response to new information or a change in focus on information we already know. But God is already aware of everything in every detail in every moment. As fully omniscient, surely his thoughts and awareness do not develop from moment to moment.

Accordingly, the image of God as angry is probably meant to help our understanding rather than presenting a literal picture of God. It is anthropomorphism, a humanizing of God that helps us catch a glimpse of something beyond our comprehension. It is God's baby talk to us in terms we can understand. The Old Testament often uses these sorts of images, like God's nose becoming red with anger or him being jealous or changing his mind.[20]

As with all such pictures, we can take the illustration too far. An example is the widespread emphasis on penal substitution (the theory that Jesus acted as a substitute to pay the penalty for our sins) in some parts of the American church today. Christians believe that God is just and will one day punish the wicked and reward the righteous. Under the influence of Paul's letter to the Romans, Western Christianity in particular has emphasized that everyone is wicked and no one is righteous. God's justice thus pushes him to punish everyone for their wrongdoing.

However, we have seen in Romans a greater emphasis on the righteousness of God or as James 2:13 puts it, that "mercy triumphs over judgment." God is both merciful and just, but the New Testament regularly sees the merciful aspect of his character as primary and the judgment aspect as secondary. We thus should reject the common picture of God as a slave to his justice. The fundamental question here is this: Did God have the authority simply to forgive us without Jesus dying on the cross or did someone have to pay for us to be forgiven?

It makes more sense for Christ's death to be understood as a *demonstration* of God's justice—which is how Romans actually states it—than as a *necessity* of God's justice. In the parable of the prodigal son in Luke 15, the father does not have to find someone to pay for the sin of the son. He has the authority simply to forgive him.[21] Any picture of God that is less than who God is in this story is skewed.

So the penal substitution view has taken the anthropomorphism of the Old Testament and a secondary emphasis of the New Testament and used them to blow the image of God's anger out of proportion. Penal substitution makes God a slave to rigid rules of justice. Someone had to pay, in this view; God could not simply forgive someone. And it had to be the party that committed the offence; no one could pay for us. So Jesus had to become human to pay the bill of justice as our representative. And, yes, every last dime of the bill had to be paid by someone.

This picture of God has little basis in the New Testament. Rather, as in the parable of the unmerciful servant (Matt. 18), God had the authority simply to wipe the slate of the servant's debt clean. In the New Testament, God sent Jesus to reveal God (John 1), preach the good news to us (Acts 10:36), free us from the slavery of death (Heb. 2:14), and, yes, die for sins (Rom. 8:3). But nowhere is the image of Jesus dying for sins developed along the lines of penal substitution.

This picture of an angry God who must be satisfied has potentially harmful implications for how we relate to others and raise our children. It can foster an unhealthy attitude, even devilish. Justice becomes the default. Wrongdoing should always have consequences, and even when a person is truly repentant for doing wrong, it can still be important for the wrongdoer to experience consequences for the sake of development. The consequences themselves somehow benefit the order of things and human nature.

I do not dispute that such consequences can be beneficial. They actually help us. But there is a difference between discipline and punishment. The legalistic sense of God's justice fosters an attitude of punishment. I know this feeling as a father; the anger of justice that can well up inside of you because of a child's open disobedience. It says, justice must be satisfied, and it pushes to immediate and swift punishment.

But Jesus' death on the cross was not a legalistic playing out of God's justice. It was a demonstration without which it would be difficult to grasp the depth of our alienation from God and of God's love for us. God was not making sure someone "gets it" so that his justice would be satisfied. God reached out to us in the most powerful way possible to show us the disorder of our world and the magnitude of setting things back in order.

Over the years as a parent, I have learned about God as I have learned to be bigger than the effrontery of disobedience. Can I see in my child's disobedience his or her need more than my offence at being disobeyed? In the public schools or in society at large, when we see defiance and wrongdoing, can we see with compassion a world that desperately needs God's help? I have come to see that a God who is out of control and must swiftly punish sin is not a big enough god. It is a Zeus.

The Christian God is not this god. The Christian God is a God who is too big not to be able to handle our disobedience. He is a God who looks on us in compassion when he sees how misguided we are to disobey and how we are hurting ourselves in our ignorance. He is big enough to take it. Indeed, he made the world in such a way that we would be able to choose whether to obey or disobey him. He is a God who disciplines to make us better, not one who punishes because he cannot help himself.

FOR FURTHER REFLECTION

1. How might the insight that what someone is saying may not be the real issue potentially help you communicate with others— or at least respond appropriately?

2. How can you tell when a question is not really a question, when it is time to listen to someone vent rather than give advice? How can you see behind the actual words of a child or another adult to what is really bothering them, things they may not be able to express or may not want to express directly?

3. What difference do you think it makes whether Paul was talking about God's righteousness being demonstrated in both judging and saving his people versus God's righteousness being a quality he transfers to believers? Do you think Paul meant the first, the second, or both? Why do you think that way?

4. Do you agree that an overemphasis on the "angry God" aspect has had a negative effect in the history of the church and even in people's lives today? How does a proper understanding of God's justice help to alleviate the potential negative effects of the "angry God" image?

3

HOW SALVATION WORKS

Over the centuries, Christians have repeatedly told themselves that the problem with the Jews was that they were trying to earn their salvation. In this scenario, it was Jesus and Paul who introduced the startling idea that we can only be saved by God's grace. The problem with this story is that it does not entirely match what we actually find in the Jewish literature of the time. And if we used this same logic, we would have to make the same accusation of the Old Testament writers. Things are not quite so simple and clear cut.

ALL HAVE SINNED

The idea that everyone sins was not original to Paul. Mainstream Jews would have agreed with him.[1] They believed that it was only because of God's grace that Israel enjoyed their special relationship with God. They did not earn this special relationship, even if God expected them to keep the Law to maintain it. And even if some Israelites failed him, God would preserve a righteous remnant within Israel forever.

So the point of disagreement was not that all had sinned, but on the implications of that sin and how God in his righteousness addressed that sin. Paul argued that Jewish sinfulness was no different from Gentile sinfulness and that Jews did not get a pass on their sins simply because they were Jews. Even more important, God determined one way to make things right with him, and it was not keeping the Jewish Law. The faithful death of Jesus Christ was the only way God would accept.

Paul spent nearly three chapters at the beginning of Romans spelling out the problem and implications of the fact that "all have sinned" (Rom. 3:23). After the usual introductory material of 1:1–15 and the key verses of 1:16–17, Paul dedicated Romans 1:18—3:20 to the sin problem of humanity both for Jews and non-Jews alike.[2] The very familiar verse, Romans 3:23, sums up this entire section: "All have sinned and are lacking the glory of God" (my translation).

The second half of this verse is often mistranslated or misunderstood. For example, one translation says, "we all fall short of God's glorious standard" (NLT) as if the problem Paul had in mind was our inability to reach God's standard of absolute perfection. But this line of thinking misses Paul's understanding of glory: Humanity lost its glory with Adam's sin, and we are regaining and will definitively regain our lost glory at the resurrection.

We can make a good argument that Psalm 8 was Paul's inspiration for this verse, especially the part that said God created humanity with the intent of crowning us "with glory and honor" (Ps. 8:5).[3] When God created humans, he put us in a position of glory and honor within the creation. But when Adam sinned, he lost that glory for all humanity. When we sin like Adam did, we demonstrate why we lack the glory God intended for all of us.

Part of our restoration—whether for believers who are alive at the time of Christ's return or for those he resurrects—involves glorification, the restoration of humanity's glory. As the book of Hebrews put it, Christ is "bringing many sons to glory" (2:10). Or as Paul put it, we are going to "share in [Christ's] glory," a "glory that will be revealed in us" (Rom. 8:17–18). Even in the meantime, we are already "being transformed into his likeness with ever-increasing glory" (2 Cor. 3:18).

Both Jews and Gentiles have lost this glory. Ever since Augustine, Christians have tended to read the *all* in "all have sinned" as referring to individuals; each and every person has sinned. And certainly Paul would agree that all individual human beings have sinned. But this is a subtle shift away from the point Paul was making, namely, that both Gentiles and Jews had sinned. In other words, *all* in this argument meant all groups; not just Gentiles, but Jews as well.[4]

When Paul said *all*, he was summarizing his argument up to that point. The kinds of sins that are mentioned in the first chapter of Romans would have caused the Jews to think of the Gentiles; these were the sins for which the Gentiles had a reputation. They "exchanged the glory of the immortal God for images made to look like mortal man and birds and animals and reptiles" (Rom. 1:23). The self-righteous Jew, like the one Paul pictured in 2:17, would have heartily agreed with Paul at this point, perhaps saying, "You preach it, Paul. Those sinful Gentiles are going to be judged!"

Paul went on to speak of men who had "abandoned natural relations with women and were inflamed with lust for one another" (1:27). Sexual immorality was another one of those stereotypical sins Jews assumed all Gentiles were doing. Homosexual sex was an example of the kinds of sexual sins a self-righteous Jew might point out to emphasize how sinful Gentiles were.

But Paul was engaged in a sting operation. Romans 2 went on to demonstrate that Jews were just as sinful as those stereotypically sinful Gentiles. In fact, Paul knew some Gentile Christians who had the law written on their hearts (2:15).[5] These Gentiles actually put the imaginary, self-righteous Jew Paul had been picturing to shame. They had "circumcised hearts," which made them truly circumcised in God's eyes, while the condemning Jew proved to be uncircumcised in heart before God (2:28–29).

So Paul's point in the first section of Romans was that God's judgment would come on all ungodliness—not only on ungodly Gentiles who worshiped idols and were sexually immoral, but on all Jews as well. All have sinned—Jews and Gentiles—and all equally face God's wrath. This is the problem we all face. And all can also equally participate in the solution: the faith of Jesus Christ.

THE FAITH OF JESUS CHRIST

In the first three chapters of Romans, especially 1:18—3:20, Paul presented the human problem. God will judge both Jew and non-Jew on the basis of how they have lived (Rom. 2:6). But both Jew and Gentile have sinned and are alienated from God. The default human situation is that both Jew and Gentile stand apart from God and are on a trajectory to receive God's judgment on the day of wrath.

In Romans 3:21—4:25, Paul laid out God's solution to this conundrum. God is a God of justice (3:25–26). I personally believe he could simply pardon all humanity on his own divine authority. But if he simply pardoned us, we would not have a clear understanding of his justice or of the serious breach of cosmic order that currently exists. So God chose to act toward the world in justice and as a faithful, saving God. The righteousness of God is wrath toward those who stand apart from him (1:18). But the righteousness of God saves and makes a path of reconciliation for those who will avail themselves.

The solution to the human sin problem is "faith in Jesus Christ" (3:22). I wonder if Paul intended a double meaning to this phrase. It could mean either the "faithfulness of Jesus Christ" or our "faith in Jesus Christ." I wonder if Paul meant the Romans to hear both. The solution to the human sin problem is the faithful obedience of Jesus to the point of death through which God atones for the sins of humanity and it is our trust in what God has done through Jesus.

In Romans 3:21–22, Paul said that God had revealed his righteousness apart from the law, namely "through faith of Jesus Christ to all who have faith" (my translation). Almost all translations render this phrase "through faith in Jesus Christ," but Paul could just as easily have meant "through the faith of Jesus." Many interpreters now take the expression that way, as one version renders it: "God's righteousness comes through the faithfulness of Jesus Christ for all who have faith in him" (CEB).[6] Paul would thus be saying that God had shown his righteousness through the faithfulness of Jesus, through Jesus' obedience unto death (see Phil. 2:8; Rom. 5:19).[7]

Human faith seems to be the major focus of what Paul said in places like Romans 4 and Galatians 3. When Paul said that "a person is justified [deemed right with God] by faith" (Rom. 3:28 NRSV), he was surely talking about a believer's faith. Paul did not seem to be talking about Jesus' faith here. He was laying down a general principle for how sinful people could be considered right with God, and the answer he gave was on the basis of their faith.

This line of thinking is apparent in Romans 4: "Blessed is the one against whom the Lord will not reckon sin" (4:8 NRSV). Paul was expanding on what it meant for God to consider someone righteous (4:6) despite their sins (4:7) and ungodliness (4:5). His train of thought was about the faith of sinful humans, not the faith of the sinless Jesus (see 2 Cor. 5:21).

Over time, I have come to also agree with those who think Paul, in both Romans and Galatians, started his argument with Jesus' faithfulness and obedience to die on the cross. Both sides have made their cases, and neither side has a silver bullet.[8]

So here is how I think Paul's argument ran in Romans 3:20–26: Neither Jew nor Gentile will be declared right with God on the day of judgment because of their keeping of the Jewish Law (3:20). In Paul's argument, works of law is more than good works. It is true that Paul did not think anyone could earn or receive a "not guilty" verdict from God on the basis of how good they were (see Rom. 4:4; 9:32). But quite likely, the phrase "works of law" would have immediately reminded a Jew of the squabbles Jewish groups had over what did or did not make a person unclean.[9] Paul said that God would not find the Gentiles worthy because of their works, and God would not find the Jews worthy just because they were circumcised and had been careful about what they ate or touched.

But God is still a righteous God. Romans 3:21 speaks of how God showed that he is righteous and in the business of saving his people. He demonstrated his righteousness in a new way, a way that did not involve the Jewish Law (the covenant rules between God and Israel). But the Law (the first five books of the Scriptures) does witness to this new way, as do the Prophets (the second half of the Jewish Bible).[10] This new way is "through the faithfulness of Jesus Christ" (3:22 CEB), that is, through the faithful, atoning death of Jesus on the cross.[11]

This new way to be right with God is available to all who have faith, both Jew and Gentile. Everyone in both groups has sinned, with the result that they lack the glory God intended for humanity (3:23). But anyone from either group can be justified or deemed right in God's eyes because of his grace. God's grace is his undeserved favor, his willingness to give us a status we do not deserve.

God has demonstrated that he is still just, that the cosmos is still in order, by offering Jesus as a sacrifice, a sign of God's own faithfulness.[12] His righteousness is proved on every side. He saves his people by providing them a path to redemption, yet he also demonstrates his justice in passing over sins (3:25–26). And God does this to everyone who has "faith in Jesus" (3:26). Those who are from the faith of Jesus are those who have been justified on the basis of Jesus' faith and who at the same time have directed their faith toward Jesus.

WHAT DOES IT MATTER?

So why does this seemingly arcane grammatical debate matter? Doesn't everyone agree that both the faithful death of Jesus and our faith in Jesus are crucial? Beyond our desire to know accurately what Paul was saying, it is mostly a matter of emphasis and tone. Nevertheless, three significant shifts result if Paul focused first on Jesus' faithfulness and then only secondly on our faith.

First, it shifts our understanding of Paul's meaning just the right amount away from our faith and back on to Jesus. The Protestant emphasis on justification by faith was an important corrective in the 1500s, but in the intervening centuries, this focus has pushed Protestants more to a me-centered path to God. Personal faith was significant for Paul, to be sure. But if Paul's initial focus was on Jesus' faithfulness, then that's where our focus should begin as well.

The Protestant emphasis has tended to foster an excessive individualism, which is out of sync with the group orientation of Paul's thought and world. The individual believer can become more the focus rather than what Jesus has done. Paul's focus was more on our corporate inclusion into Christ and what he has done rather than on what we do as individuals, though, again, the individual's role is significant.

A second shift is from focusing our faith on Jesus to focusing it on God the Father. Paul spoke of placing our faith in Jesus (for example, Rom. 9:33), and directing our faith toward him remains a crucial element in Romans 3:22 and Galatians 2:16 no matter how one takes the phrase "faith of Jesus." But a careful look at what Paul said elsewhere reveals a consistent priority of placing our faith in God the Father. After every knee bows (Phil. 2:11), after everything is put under Jesus' feet (1 Cor. 15:28), God the Father is the one to whom Jesus is servant and subject.

Throughout Romans 4, God is the object of faith. God justifies the ungodly (Rom. 4:5), and calls into existence things that did not exist (4:17). He raised Jesus from the dead (4:24). Christians understand Jesus to be God, "eternally begotten of the Father," as the Nicene Creed of A.D. 381 would later put it. So we sometimes fail to distinguish the unique emphasis of Paul's writings at his stage in the flow of revelation. The "faith of Jesus" interpretation seems closer to Paul's emphasis regarding where faith should be directed. Yes, faith was to be directed toward Christ, but only secondarily. For Paul, faith was primarily directed toward God the Father.

Finally, the "faith of Jesus" interpretation reveals a Paul who was interested in the life and humanity of Jesus and not only his death. Because we rightly believe Jesus to be the second person of the Trinity, it is easy to forget that he was fully human. Paul and the New Testament authors did not have this problem. The author of Hebrews, for example, spoke of Jesus learning obedience through the things he suffered (Heb. 5:8) and being tempted like us (4:15).

None of these shifts proves beyond the shadow of a doubt that the "faith of Jesus" interpretation of Romans 3:22 is correct. But the shifts do show that this interpretation fits better with Paul's context and the statements he made elsewhere, particularly that faith was primarily directed toward God the Father. This view puts the focus of justification more on Jesus than on us as individuals. And it appropriately includes the human struggle and obedient action of Jesus in the equation of salvation.

LIFE REFLECTIONS

Christians have drawn on a number of images over the years to get at the significance of Jesus' death on the cross. Unlike Christian beliefs about Jesus, the church never settled on just one picture of the atonement he provided. He satisfied God's anger. He took our place. He showed us God's love and how to obey. He defeated the evil powers that rule this age. These are all lenses through which Christians at different times have explained what Jesus did on the cross. All have truth to them.

But the image that I think might speak most to our current age is reconciliation. In a broken world where AIDS has left thousands of orphans in Africa, we understand the longing for a father. In America where children are as likely to grow up in a broken home as in one where their parents have been together their whole lives, we understand alienation and distance. We understand brokenness and the need for reconciliation. Some of the images Christians have used throughout the centuries may have strong links to other times. But how many of us have ever seen a sacrifice? We understand alienation and the need for reconciliation.

Atonement is reconciliation that takes place because of a sacrifice, an offering. God himself made the sacrifice. Jesus gave himself as the offering so that we might be reconciled to God (see 2 Cor. 5:18–19). The righteousness of God in the book of Romans is God's propensity to reach out and rescue his people and, indeed, the world. In a world of profound alienation, this message still rings out as immensely good news!

FOR FURTHER REFLECTION

1. How would thinking of "getting saved" in terms of a lifetime of faithfulness leading to God's ultimate salvation change the way you go about your Christian life?

2. What is the balance between faith and works? Between our part and God's part?

3. Many Christians picture God's expectations for us as unattainable. Because they have an excessive sense of God's justice, they abandon any real sense of God's expectation from us at all. Do you agree with the above assessment? How might a more balanced sense of God's expectation change our attitudes toward our lives?

4. If we tend to be too individualistic in our focus, what do you think a more balanced sense of our place in the Christian community would look like?

4

THE HUMAN CONDITION

THE SECOND SECTION OF ROMANS

The first major section of Romans presented Jesus Christ as God's solution to the sin problem that all humanity, both Jew and non-Jew, have. Paul summed up the entire situation with the key verses of Romans (1:16–17). Then he unfolded the coming judgment of God on everyone (1:18 — 3:20) with no one, not even the most law-observant Jew, good enough to escape on the basis of his or her own goodness. Then Paul presented God's gracious solution: faith in what God has done through Christ, the only God-appointed solution (3:21 — 4:25).

The result is that, "since we have been justified through faith, we have peace with God through our Lord Jesus Christ" (5:1). Our trust in what God has done through Jesus — "through whom we have gained access by faith into this grace in which we now stand" (5:2) — has led

God to declare us right with him, to justify us. We are now at peace with God. We are not facing the wrath of God, "being revealed from heaven against all the godlessness and wickedness" of humanity (1:18). "Since we have now been justified by his blood, how much more shall we be saved from God's wrath through him!" (5:9).

God did not have to do any of these things. He had no obligation to humanity to fix its problem. What he did through Christ was rather a demonstration of his righteousness (1:17; 3:25–26). The actions of Christ and God were so inextricably intertwined that Paul moved from one to the other without pause: God demonstrated his love toward us in the fact that while we were ungodly sinners, Christ died for us (5:6–8).

Romans 5–8 unpacks some of the implications of what God did through Christ. The first verses of Romans 5 give a quick summary of the new situation: We have been reconciled to God. The second half of Romans 5 then places what Christ did into historical perspective.[1] Christ's act of obedience corresponds to the disobedient act of the first human, Adam. Adam caused the sin problem with his act of sin. Christ solved the sin problem with his act of faith (see Rom. 5:19).

Romans 6–7 addresses the role of the Jewish Law. If only Christ's death makes a person right with God, what is the place of the Jewish Law? Why did God institute it in the first place? And if we are not truly judged by the law, then can we continue sinning just as before, only without any consequences? These chapters can be very confusing, and may have been confusing to the original audience (see 2 Pet. 3:15–16). Paul's answer was that the law made us ready for Christ and that Christ now enables us to keep its essence, which we were not able to do when under the law.

Romans 8 puts it all together in a triumphal celebration of freedom from condemnation and looks forward to the final redemption of our bodies and the whole creation. Christ made us right with God who wants to give life to our mortal bodies even while we are still on earth (Rom. 8:11–13). But we especially look forward to the coming redemption of our bodies and the whole creation when Christ returns (8:22–23). Regardless of current suffering, nothing can compare to what is to come (8:18).

ADAM'S FAMILY

Paul only explicitly discussed Adam for about ten verses in Romans 5, along with a couple verses in 1 Corinthians 15. The significance some Christians find in these verses is disproportionately large to the attention Adam received in Paul's own writings and the Bible as a whole. It is understandable that later Christians would focus on them, because Paul pointed to Adam as the reason why sin and death are in the world.

First Corinthians 15:22 puts Paul's thinking on death succinctly: "For as in Adam all die, so in Christ all will be made alive." Because of Adam, all human beings die. This astoundingly brief comment, along with its more detailed explanation in Romans 5, has had immense influence on key Christian thinkers like Augustine and John Calvin. And their interpretation of these passages has influenced the majority of Christians today. Adam introduced death into the world by introducing sin into the world: "sin entered the world through one man, and death through sin" (Rom. 5:12).

Paul's sense of how this process worked is vague to us today. Perhaps the best explanation is that Paul saw sin as a power that came over the creation as a result of Adam's disobedient act in the garden of Eden. Paul believed that Adam's sinful act somehow caused the rest of humanity to end up as sinners. Paul said in Romans 5:19, "Through the disobedience of the one man the many were made sinners." In some way that Paul never really explained, Adam introduced into the world the "law of sin and death" (8:2). The result was a "law at work in the members of my body" (7:23), so that "death came to all men, because all sinned" (5:12).

But Paul indicated that this power somehow enslaved the rest of the physical realm as well. Again, Paul was not clear about how it specifically works, but it would seem that God subjected the rest of the material world to corruption and decay at the same time humanity came under the power of sin (see Rom. 8:20). Similarly, Paul believed that the rest of creation would be freed from decay at the same time that our physical bodies are transformed—either by resurrection or when Christ returns from heaven.

Later Christians took these brief comments of Paul and developed them further according to their own understanding of psychology and the world. Augustine in particular crafted Paul's thoughts into a highly developed system. For example, Augustine read Paul to teach the total depravity of humanity—the idea that human beings cannot do anything good at all in their own power. Paul never made such an absolute statement, so if Augustine was right, it was a God-inspired development of Christian understanding. Most of the Western church later followed Augustine's lead. In my opinion, the Eastern church remained closer to Paul's understanding, sensing the thoroughness of human fallenness but without invoking such absolute terms.

Paul told the Romans that all had sinned, by which he meant both Jew and Gentile. It is true that Paul also thought that every individual had sinned as well (see 3:19), but that was not his focus. Further, Paul told the Romans that the world was under the power of sin, which made it impossible for us mortals in our default condition not to sin (see 7:19). But it was Augustine who universalized and systematized these ideas, lifting them out of Paul's Jew-Gentile debate and focusing on the individual.

When Paul said that no good dwelt in his flesh (7:18), he also spoke of having a will to do good (7:19). In other words, Paul believed there could be good in your spirit.[2] He said that the power of sin in us made us "utterly sinful" (7:13), but Paul was talking about how many sin acts the power of sin causes in a person, not about whether any good is left at all. Romans 3:10–18 is meant to paint a picture of the sinfulness of humanity. Indeed, none of the verses Paul quoted from the Old Testament originally meant that every person had sinned, let alone that no good at all existed in humanity.

In short, you will not find in any statement of Paul that God had left no good in humanity at all. It was Augustine who took Paul's teaching one step further, with Calvin and Wesley following closely behind. Perhaps they were inspired to read Paul this way. But the Eastern church seems a little closer to Paul's original thought, having a strong sense of the thoroughness of human sinfulness, but stopping short of absolute statements about whether there might be any goodness in humanity at all.

REINTERPRETING GENESIS

Christian interpretations of Genesis 2–3 today are also an interesting mixture of reinterpretation piled on reinterpretation, like a wall that has been painted over several times without completely removing the previous paint. For example, we do not find anywhere in the biblical text the idea that the "image of God," mentioned in Genesis 1:27, has either been marred or destroyed.[3] The story of Adam and Eve's sin in Genesis 3 never mentions the image of God being damaged or destroyed, and Paul himself never said it was in any way. This idea comes entirely from later Christian tradition. It may point to a truth, but it was never articulated in the Bible.

The concept of Adam's sin being the fall or the original sin also comes from Augustine rather than the Bible. *The fall* is a short-hand term for the event of Adam's sin that resulted in humanity and creation being under the power of sin and subject to decay. Adam's sin is thus the first or original sin. But Augustine and later Western Christian tradition meant more by these terms than Paul himself, and we can call much of it into question.

For example, Augustine and many Christians since have believed that we have the guilt of Adam's sin hanging over our heads. Many mainline traditions consider infant baptism necessary to cleanse a child of the guilt of Adam's original sin. While I have no problem with infant baptism, this particular view of it has no relation to the Bible's teaching about Adam's sin.[4] Romans 5:12 only said that death passed on us because we all sinned like Adam, not that we all die as part of the penalty for Adam's sin. Paul said we all die because we all sin.[5]

Similarly, the original NIV and other Bible versions introduce later interpretations into Paul's writing when they translate Paul's word *flesh* with the phrase "sinful nature" or, as some refer to it, "carnal nature."[6] The skew here is to introduce the word *nature* into the discussion, which Paul never used in this context. The flesh for Paul clearly related to the skin, since that is the starting point for understanding the word. But Paul also said that "those who are in the flesh cannot please God" (8:8 NRSV). Paul sometimes used the word *flesh* in a morally neutral way (see Rom. 1:3 NRSV, KJV, NASB, ESV). But he could also use it of that part of us that makes us lose in our struggle against sin (see Rom. 7:5).

For Paul, flesh was the body, the material part of a person, the part that belongs to this creation. For this reason, it is the part of a person that is particularly susceptible to the power of sin in this world.[7] For Paul, those in Christ received the Spirit, and the Spirit living inside a person meant that he or she should no longer be in the flesh but in the Spirit.

Talk of a sinful or carnal (fleshly) nature has led to all sorts of rabbit trails. Some Christians have taken Paul's metaphor and extended the imagery to worlds unknown. Thinking of the sinful nature as a thing inside a person, some debated whether the thing might be eradicated or only suppressed. If it could be eradicated, how might it ever come back? But if only suppressed, then what did that say about the power of God over sin? But Paul thought about it in terms of powers over the body. A person either remained under the power of sin—the default state of the flesh given the current age—or became a slave to righteousness under the power of the Holy Spirit.

Paul expanded on the Genesis text, which did not use words like *condemnation* or *disobedience*. Paul added this larger perspective to the story. Genesis explains why men have to work so hard tilling the soil, women have such pain giving birth to children, and humans and snakes do not get along (Gen. 3:15 in its original meaning).[8] Since Adam and Eve had to eat from the Tree of Life to live forever (3:22), the Genesis story described human death as a result of their actions but not the cause of death itself. Death is apparently the default existence of creatures.

Some other aspects of the story come from later interpretations rather than Genesis itself. Not until the first century before Christ was there evidence of anyone thinking the serpent was Satan.[9] Indeed, Jewish understanding of Satan apparently did not appear until well after the Jews returned from the Babylonian captivity in 538 B.C.[10] Further, the specific consequences regarding the soil and the pains of childbirth fall short of Paul's more systemic subjugation of the creation to corruption. Here again, this dimension comes from Paul rather than from the Genesis text.

LIFE REFLECTIONS

So what do we take for life from all these layers of interpretation today? One benefit we can get from analyzing the meanings and reinterpretations is clarity. We can see the earlier meanings from the later ones and prayerfully consider which ones are of God and which have more to do with specific moments in history. It gives us clearer choices to make together as believers, even if the landscape becomes more complex.

Contemporary culture brings additional factors to consider. For example, the nearly unanimous consensus of scientists is that the universe is very old and that complex life evolved over time from simpler forms. Could virtually the entire scientific community be wrong? Certainly they have been before—on whether the sun goes around the earth, on whether time is a fixed framework, and on whether space is continuous and infinite. But when we realize how much more there is to understanding Paul and Genesis than we might have thought, we need to at least consider whether the biblical basis for opposing evolution is as firm as we might think. What if God directed in some way an evolutionary process similar to what many scientists think? This is the option known as theistic evolution, a view that sees evolution as God's way of creating humanity.

The point is that we should think carefully about the options rather than simply closing discussion. We certainly do not want to compromise to make the world think better of Christians or for any other reason, but we should also be fully aware of our own limitations, including the fact that our fallen minds affect our understanding of the Bible just as much as our fallen understanding of anything else. Would the authority or truthfulness of Genesis 1 be any less if it were a poetic presentation of God as sole creator of an orderly world rather than a straightforward blow-by-blow documentary?

Romans 5 and 1 Corinthians 15 pose a greater challenge, as Paul apparently argued that death and the decay of the world entered as a result of Adam's sin. Some Christian scientists, convinced by the evidence of their field as they understand it, strategize possible reinterpretations of Paul. Perhaps he meant spiritual death entered through Adam, not physical death. Perhaps he actually understood it as Genesis does, that everything would have died anyway. Perhaps it was only the fact that Adam and Eve did not get to eat from the Tree of Life that resulted in death.

Keep in mind that we regularly shift over time in what passages we emphasize and do not emphasize, usually without realizing it. For example, at one point in my life, passages in the Bible against women adorning themselves with jewelry caught my attention (1 Pet. 3:3). An earring was a big deal to me. Given where I was raised, it seemed impossible that a woman could wear one without it being a big deal. I now laugh about that, knowing that most women are about as prideful to wear an earring as I might be when I try to match my shirt and pants.

Should we labor so hard with a specific reading of this handful of five to ten verses? After all, the arguments of the Bible were always made in the categories of their original authors and audiences—otherwise God would not have gotten his message across. Paul's point was that Christ abolished death for all those who trust in him. To make this point, he drew on one contemporary understanding of Genesis. His point had to do with the Romans more than with history and certainly more than with science. It was atheistic evolution and its social consequences that alarmed some Christians in the early twentieth century.[11] Before then, many godly Christians had tried to determine whether some form of theistic evolution might be compatible with the Bible and Christianity, as many godly Christian scientists do today.

So let those Christian scientists who are competent debate the evidence both for and against theistic evolution. Let us remember that science is often wrong and has been known to change its mind many times on a massive scale. But let us also remember that the biblical texts themselves are not without their own ambiguity, and that the Spirit has often instructed, corrected, and trained in righteousness through figurative interpretations. What will only hinder faith in the long run is if we pretend we have it all sorted out and that everyone who disagrees with us is an infidel.

Another area where modern study potentially impacts our discussions is in the area of brain research and psychology. Neuroscientists still have a long way to go in mapping the brain, but it seems fairly clear that there is at least some part of the brain that corresponds to each human experience. Whether thought, memory, anger, personality, or even religious experience, we can say which parts of the brain are active when that happens. Change the structure of the brain—whether through neurological disease, cancer, or physical injury—and you change the person.

These discoveries have led some Christians to explore whether the idea of the soul might be an instance of Christian language that points to something real but not exactly in the way we have thought.[12] Such Christians point out that the word *soul* in the Old Testament never refers to a detachable part of a person that survives death. Rather, the Hebrew word *soul* refers to an entire living thing, whether a human or a fish. Even in the New Testament, it is only rarely that the word *soul* seems to refer to a part of my human makeup (see Heb. 4:12). Our common conceptions of the soul have as much to do with later Greek influence on Christianity as with what the Bible actually says.

My intention is not to take a position on this issue here. My point is that if scholars are debating on this level, then we can see how far astray the old arguments about whether our carnal nature can be eradicated or suppressed were. Yet no one who pays much attention to the world around us will doubt that our world is thoroughly enslaved to sin. Ask the social worker at the local elementary school, the prosecutor at the courthouse, the nurse at the emergency room, or the person who helps with foreign aid. They will no doubt strongly attest to the feeling of Romans 3:10: "There is no one righteous, not even one." Godliness and righteousness are indeed a miracle from God in this world.

FOR FURTHER REFLECTION

1. Do you agree that Christians have at times inappropriately taken stories or metaphors Paul told and made them into rigid systems of ideas? Can you think of any areas where you have potentially done the same with Christian ideas? What can happen when we lose sight of the key points and principles and become entangled in the details of playing them out?

2. How important do you think it is for Christians to believe that we have a detachable part of us we call the soul? Could this be another picture pointing to truths God could accomplish in other ways, or is it essential that we take the idea of the soul literally?

3. Does it bother you that many of those who are competent in science believe strongly that complex life on earth evolved from a simpler form? How do you process this issue as a Christian? If you are open to the possibility, how do you relate this issue with your faith? If you are closed to the possibility, how do you relate this issue with your use of computers, cell phones, and airplanes?

5

THE PURPOSE OF THE LAW

Paul's comments on the law in his letters have so confused those who have studied them that there are countless books and articles on the subject. The key is to realize that Paul uses the word *law* in several different ways. Because he slid from one to the other without notice, it is easy to see why Christians have interpreted him so differently.

CONTINUE SINNING?

Paul used a question-and-answer (or diatribe) style earlier in Romans to raise possible objections to his way of thinking and then to answer them. He resumed this approach in Romans 6, which began a section that dealt with one of the main objections to his teaching. People were parodying him as if he were teaching, "Let us do evil that good may result."

Paul attacked this false accusation head-on. "Shall we go on sinning so that grace may increase?" (Rom. 6:1). "Shall we sin because we are not under law but under grace?" (6:15). Paul's answer in both cases was an emphatic no: "By no means!" (6:2, 15).

In truth, no mainstream interpreter of Paul has ever accepted the old parody of Luther, "Sin boldly that grace may come." Thanks to my colleague, Dr. Chris Bounds, I know that Luther never made this statement and no support for such an approach to sin from any mainstream Lutheran, Reformed, Baptist, Methodist, or any other major Reformation tradition can be found. Christian groups may differ in their definitions of sin. They may differ in how much they think a Christian will normally sin. But no tradition worthy of the name Christian teaches that Christians will continue to sin no differently than before they received the Holy Spirit.

Romans 7:13–25 can confuse matters in this discussion, mostly because we have a difficult time following how Paul used the same words in different ways. So many of us identify with the words in 7:19: "For what I do is not the good I want to do; no, the evil I do not want to do—this I keep on doing." We latch on to this sentiment because it seems to fit our personal experience. In the process, we inadvertently ignore the overall context in which Paul made his argument. It is perhaps the single greatest misunderstanding of Paul's writings, as common as it is wrong.

In context, Paul's argument had pushed him to his single most vulnerable point. Why had God instituted the Jewish Law in the first place if, as Paul was arguing, it was not an effective path to God? Paul said that Gentiles did not have to observe the parts of it that were Jew-specific, such as circumcision. And he said that Jews were not able to be right with God on the basis of how well they kept the law. But he also said that getting right with God through grace was no excuse to sin, to "do wrong." And the definition of doing wrong came from the law.

This line of thinking is confusing to us today, and it may have also been confusing to the Romans as well. It makes us want to ask Paul what the law was good for since he said we are not under it (1 Cor. 9:20) and do not violate it (Rom. 3:31). He implied it had never been effective, so why did God institute it in the first place? These sorts of questions no doubt led Paul to write Romans 7, where he explained the role of the law in God's plan and how it applied to believers.

I am convinced that a great deal of our confusion comes from the fact that Paul glided seamlessly between a number of different meanings for the word *law* in Romans and Galatians. Perhaps a good place to start is to remember that the Law in general was the Torah, the Pentateuch, the first five books of our Old Testament. When Paul said that the "Law and the Prophets" witnessed recent developments (Rom. 3:21), he was referring to the first five books of Scripture, a body of literature.

When we ask what Paul meant by sin, we are led quickly to the Jewish Law. Paul said in Romans 5:13 that sin was not reckoned where there was no law, even though sin was present. This comment makes it clear that one purpose of the Jewish Law was to identify exactly what sin was. Paul confirmed this purpose a little later in Romans 7:7 when he said, "I would not have known what sin was except through the law. For I would not have known what coveting really was if the law had not said, 'Do not covet.'"

DEFINING SIN AND LAW

A key observation here is that Paul nowhere offered an absolute definition of sin. Sin was not missing the mark for Paul, as if anything short of absolute perfection was sin. Sin was, in one respect, to violate the Jewish Law, where the law was a record of the actions that are wrong. As we might expect of the Old Testament, such violations were far more concrete than abstract. They were not some introspective flub where a less-than-perfect thought flew through your head. I suspect that even when Jesus spoke of looking at another woman with lust (Matt. 5:28), there was a level of intent to act that went well beyond what most today would call a lustful thought.

A great starter definition of the verb *to sin* is "to do wrong," where wrongdoing is defined in the Jewish Law. Closely related is to wrong another person, as in sinning against someone (see Matt. 18:21; 1 Cor. 8:12). Such definitions know nothing of the common sentiment that we "sin every day in word, thought, and deed." This sentiment regarding sin does not come from the Bible but later Christian theology. The Bible consistently treats acts of sin or wrongdoing as things that are avoidable and bad.

Paul did not use the word *sin* in reference to every part of the Jewish Law. Paul never spoke of someone who touched a dead body as sinning, nor did he say that someone who worked on the Sabbath sinned. He likely did not consider such actions to be sins for a believer, especially a Gentile believer.[1] We therefore encounter the key ambiguity in Paul's rhetoric about the Jewish Law. Sometimes he used the word *law* in reference to parts of the law he did not apply to Gentile believers, while at other times, he used the word in reference to parts of the law that still applied to believers. But, he did not clearly distinguish in his language between the two.

In the first volume of this series, *Paul—Messenger of Grace*, I argued that when Paul used the phrase "works of law" in Galatians, he primarily had in mind those parts of the Jewish Law that distinguished Jew from Gentile.[2] In Galatians, circumcision was the key issue under discussion when Paul said, "No one will be justified by the works of the law" (Gal. 2:16 NRSV). The argument of Romans was more general.

Certainly Paul did not think anyone could earn God's favor, but the key subject in Romans was whether a Jew had any advantage over a non-Jew in being right with God. The underlying issue was not, "Can you be good enough for God to accept you?" It was, "Is there something about being a Jew that automatically makes you right with God?"

So when Paul said he was not under the law (see 1 Cor. 9:20) and that right standing with God did not come by "works of law" (see Rom. 3:28), he was thinking primarily of things like circumcision, Jewish food and purity laws, and Sabbath laws. As part of that argument, he made general statements about the impossibility of earning a right standing with God (see 4:4–5; 9:32). But these were supporting points, not the main one. When Paul distanced believers from the law, he primarily had the Jew-specific aspects of the Jewish Law in view, the boundary type laws that distinguished Jew from Gentile.

What is confusing is that Paul also talked about the law with a very different content in view. Sometimes he had a certain core law in view that was universal and timeless. When he talked in Romans 2:14 about Gentiles who "do by nature things required by the law," he could not have been referring to Jew-specific elements, because Gentiles by definition do not do such things. Paul could only have had a universal, moral core in mind. It was this part of the Jewish Law that Paul had in mind in Romans 6–8.

NO LONGER SLAVES TO SIN

The key to understanding Romans 6–8 is to understand the before and after images Paul repeatedly presented throughout the section. The first is in 6:17–18: "But thanks be to God that, though you used to be slaves to sin, you wholeheartedly obeyed the form of teaching to which you were entrusted. You have been set free from sin and have become slaves to righteousness."

Notice the timing. The Romans used to be slaves to sin before they believed. Then they became free from sin and slaves to righteousness. Paul gave no middle ground. A person is either a slave to righteousness or a slave to sin. You are not both at the same time. The timing for Paul was not ambiguous. Before you commit to Christ, you are a slave to sin. After you believe, you are not to "let sin reign in your mortal body so that you obey its evil desires" (6:12).

Paul gave a similar contrast in 6:19–22 and again in 7:5–6. His statement in Romans 7:5–6 is worth noting, because it led to what he would say later in the chapter: "For while we *were* in the flesh, the sinful passions, which were aroused by the Law, were at work in the members of our body to bear fruit for death. *But now we have been released* from the Law, having died to that by which we were bound, so that we serve in newness of the Spirit" (NASB, emphasis added).

Again, the timing is clear. Being "in the flesh" is a matter of a believer's past. And the "fruit for death" that Paul had in mind is also clear from the previous chapter. Romans 6:19 put it clearly: "you *used to* offer the parts of your body in slavery to impurity and to ever-increasing wickedness, so *now* offer them in slavery to righteousness leading to holiness" (emphasis added). And when Paul said we have "been released from the Law," he was not talking about some legal technicality or sleight of hand where God treats us like we have become righteous even though we continue sinning as before. Such an interpretation is not consistent with what Paul said in the previous chapter.

There is no ambiguity. Paul said we were slaves to sin. We used to act in ways that led to death. Paul said believers no longer let their sinful passions control their actions. Believers are set free from the law of sin.

Romans 8 confirms this same train of thought one more time: "the law of the Spirit of life in Christ Jesus has *set you free* from the law of sin and of death . . . so that the requirement of the Law *might be fulfilled* in us who do not walk according to the flesh but according to the Spirit" (8:2, 4 NASB, emphasis added). *Walking* is the Jewish word for how one lives (*halakah*), confirming that Paul was not talking about something only figuratively fulfilled in us. He was talking about believers actually keeping the essence of the law, like the Gentiles he mentioned in Romans 2:15 who demonstrated the law written on their hearts.[3]

So Paul's thoughts in Romans 6–8 seem quite clear. One is either a slave to sin or a slave to righteousness. Before the Spirit, a person is a slave to sin, with the result that he or she acts sinfully and follows the lead of the sinful passions inside. After the Spirit, however, a person is set free from the law of sin and becomes a slave to righteousness, with the result that he or she acts righteously and actually fulfills the righteous requirement of the Jewish Law.

It is only when we have this context firmly in mind that we should approach Romans 7:14–25. The popular interpretation of these verses is so deeply ingrained in the contemporary Christian's mind that it will take every effort to keep most readers from throwing out Paul's earlier thoughts. Because of what he said before and after, Paul could not have been saying that he was still a slave to sin or that he continued to be unable to keep the heart of the Jewish Law unless he was saying he was not a believer.

"We know that the law is spiritual; but I am unspiritual, sold as a slave to sin" (7:14). Paul could not have been talking about himself at that very moment because he had clearly, repeatedly, and emphatically said that believers used to be slaves to sin but are now free (6:17–22; 7:5–6; 8:1–4). If Paul was talking about the default state of the Christian or himself, then his train of thought was fundamentally incoherent.

The only way Romans 7 could be understood this way would be to rip it completely from its context of the letter.

The only way to read Romans 7:14–25 coherently is to see Paul putting himself into the shoes of the Jew who has not yet believed, not yet been baptized into Christ, and not yet received the Spirit.[4] It is a person who "wants to do good" (7:21 NASB) but is incapable because he or she is a slave to sin. In short, Paul was not talking about his current experience but explaining what the purpose of the law was even though unbelieving Jews were unable to keep it.[5]

Paul's theology would have starkly raised the question of the law among Jews. Paul said that keeping the Jewish Law did not make a Jew right with God. Only the death of Christ and faith in what God had done through Christ's death could make a person right with him. The purpose of the law, which Paul stated clearly in Romans and Galatians, was to show the need for Christ (see Gal. 3:24).

Romans 7:14–25 presents this need dramatically. Here's how the logic goes: I am a Jew; I want to keep the Jewish Law, and it tells me what God desires of me (meaning those core parts that apply universally); but I find in my default state that I am unable to keep it. I discover that I am a slave to sin, that I am "utterly sinful" (7:13). Who will free me from this body that makes me do things that lead to death?

"Thanks be to God—through Jesus Christ our Lord!" (Rom. 7:25). That is to say, when I am incorporated into Christ, I am set free from this horrible default state in which all humanity finds itself, both Jews and Gentiles. This exuberant exclamation, "Thanks be to God," is also in Romans 6:17. Paul's thoughts here are exactly the same as before: "thanks be to God that, though you used to be slaves to sin, you wholeheartedly obeyed the form of teaching to which you were entrusted. You have been set free from sin and have become slaves to righteousness" (6:17–18).[6]

So in Romans 8, Paul returned to much the same point he had reached at the beginning of Romans 5, where he talked about peace with God (Rom. 5:1) after his lengthy discussion of the need and basis for justification in the first four chapters. Romans 8:1 returns to this point of "no condemnation" after more than two chapters on the problem of overcoming sin in a person's life. The rest of Romans 8 celebrates the benefits of the Spirit's power in the believer, both now and in the redemption that is to come.

REDEMPTION IS COMING

Romans 8 was truly a climax in Paul's letter. The first four chapters presented the problem of God's coming wrath on all humanity, coupled with the solution of faith in what God had done through Jesus Christ. The first part of the fifth chapter celebrated justification and peace with God on the basis of faith and the blood of Jesus. The last part of Romans 5–7 looked at the human condition from a different vantage point. We used to be enslaved to sin, and the Jewish Law only unveiled our helpless state. Who will free us from our bodies enslaved to sin? "Thanks be to God," Paul exclaimed, "through Jesus Christ our Lord!" (7:25).

Romans 8 begins like Romans 5, with the believer's glorious situation. We are freed from the condemnation of the Jewish Law and the law of sin and death. The law of the Spirit has set us free from the law of sin and death. The Jewish Law was not able to accomplish this feat, as Paul explained in Romans 7. The weakness of our human flesh was unable to keep the law, even in its essence. But God sent Jesus in human flesh, like ours, only not under the power of sin. And Christ's blameless sin offering put an end to sinfulness.

The result is that we are now able to walk in newness of life (see Rom. 6:4). Those who walk, not according to the power of sin over our flesh, but according to the power of the Spirit, are now actually able to meet the righteous requirement of the Jewish Law. Gentiles demonstrate the work of the law written on their hearts and do the things of the law (2:14–15). Again, Paul did not refer here to the same part of the law that he elsewhere argued believers did not need to keep (see Gal. 4:10, 21). He did not mean Jew-specific things like circumcision, but the essence of the law, Christ's law (see 1 Cor. 9:21).

The essence of it for Paul was that those who are "controlled by the sinful nature" cannot please God (Rom. 8:8). The flesh—our skin under the power of sin—is not able to do the good we want to do (8:7), as Paul vividly portrayed in Romans 7. The flesh is hostile toward God. The only way to please God is to get out of our flesh by getting "in the Spirit" (8:9 NASB). If we live according to the flesh, our destiny is eternal death (8:12–13). The only path to life is to put to death the deeds of the flesh and be led by the Spirit. This entire argument is thoroughly oriented around living or "walking." Paul was not giving an abstract, sophisticated fiction about living sinfully while being considered legally righteous. His wording was about how we live and what we do in this life.

The secret is the Spirit. If someone does not have the Holy Spirit, Paul said he or she is not even a Christian (8:9). The Spirit inside us brings death to our sinful bodies, and we are deemed righteous or justified by God (8:10). We are buried with Christ in baptism and die with him (6:4). The miracle is that we not only are deemed righteous by God, but also that the Spirit then raises our mortal bodies so that we can live righteously (8:11). We rise with Christ so that we can walk in newness of life (6:4).

LIFE REFLECTIONS

So it would seem, after working through Romans 6–8, that Paul taught sin is not a normal part of a believer's life, despite justification by faith. Indeed, this is exactly the accusation he tried to fight. Rumors circulated that he taught, "Let us do evil that good may result" (Rom. 3:8). People said Paul taught that sin was a good thing. He worked hard in Romans 6–8 to show that the accusation was false. His message was that we cannot continue sinning (6:2, 15), that those who are "in the flesh" cannot please God (8:8 NASB).

But after we have finally heard Paul in his own words and shaken off the popular misinterpretation of Romans 7, we are still left with the problem of application. The reason Christians have been able to ignore Paul's repeated statements on sin in Romans 6–8 is because they identify so much with the second half of Romans 7: "For what I want to do I do not do, but what I hate I do" (7:15). Experience trumps the surrounding two chapters. How then do we deal with the pervasive sense of sin so many have in their lives?

In this regard, the Wesleyan tradition has always been more optimistic than other traditions. Historically, we have preached and taught that God can perform miracles in one's spiritual life just as he can and often does with physical sickness. But a desire for holiness, as our tradition has called this hope, can also degenerate into petty legalism over what people wear or how they do their hair. At times, some who spoke most about holiness were, ironically, most sinful in their attitude toward others and did little that was positive in the wider world.

Our pessimism regarding the possibility of holiness stems partly from how introspective our world has become. We are more aware of our feelings and internal motivations than any generation in any time or place prior to the 1800s. Christians have fully absorbed Jesus' identification of the heart as the source of our actions and Paul's prioritization of faith over works. Indeed, we probably experience these emphases more intensely than Jesus and Paul meant when they spoke them, and we can hyper-analyze our motives well beyond anything they probably intended. Our standard of living above sin goes far beyond the biblical expectations. We think anything short of absolute perfection is sin. The New Testament standard is much closer to John Wesley's understanding of sin as intentionally doing wrong.[7]

Then there are addictions and tendencies. Our strengths often have corresponding weaknesses. Decisive and assertive leaders, for example, can have a tendency to run over people. Those who are compassionate and understanding can have a tendency to enable others lack of discipline or to empower their weaknesses. Sometimes people develop addictions they could never overcome in their own power. We have developed a keen sense of these sorts of things in the last two centuries of introspection. While the New Testament spoke of slavery to sin, its world did not consider the role of genetics and environment in the sin equation.

Paul's argument against sin in Romans 6–8 was a defensive one. He made it clear that his theology did not encourage or excuse sin. Because he taught a person could not get right with God by keeping the law (focusing on the Jew-specific parts), he needed to make it clear that he was not excusing the violation of what we often call the moral law.[8] But that debate was far removed from the issue we are discussing now; namely, to what extent is sin a normal part of a Christian's life?

The book of 1 John had the mix just right. People who think they have never sinned do not understand the human condition (1 John 1:8, 10). Yet intentionally doing wrong cannot be normal for a Christian. After all, we have God's "seed" inside us (3:9). Nevertheless, Christians do sin and when this happens, we need to seek God's forgiveness through Jesus Christ (2:1).

Romans 8 ends on a triumphant note, which is a fitting end to the first eight chapters of the letter (especially Rom. 1:16—8:39). Paul reflected on the believer's current situation in contrast to the one that is coming. He and other Christians were suffering, but a "glory" was coming (8:18). If the default state of humanity is that "all have sinned and are lacking the glory of God" (3:23, my translation), then those in Christ look forward to a "glory that will be revealed" (8:17–18).

Christ set in motion the complete solution to the problem Adam's sin created. Our sins can already be forgiven. We can already be considered innocent in God's divine court. The Spirit can already give life to our mortal bodies here and now so that we can walk in newness of life. But we still await the complete redemption of the creation, currently enslaved to corruption and decay (8:21), and we await our full attainment of the glory of God lost through sin.

This is where Paul connected the enslavement of human flesh to that of the material creation. Of course he would connect these, because in his way of thinking, they are made of the same weak materials. They are both subject to spiritual powers, whether to the power of sin as they currently are or to the power of the Spirit as they can and will be.

Our flesh or skin, the part of us that belongs to this world, will always be our weakest point. It is not a matter of eradicating or suppressing a sinful nature. It is a matter of whether we are controlled by the Spirit. If we are controlled by the Spirit, then the power of sin over our flesh is dead. But the weakness of our flesh and its potential to sin is always as close as our loss of the Spirit.

In our current situation, embodied in weakness and potentially empowered in Spirit, we will always face potential struggles. Some of these come from the world around us. But if we neglect our connection to the Holy Spirit, they will come from our bodies as well. We have two powerful intercessors in our fight. Christ's atonement has already interceded for our justification at God's right hand (8:34). But the Spirit gives constant intercession for us as well, even beyond what we know we need (8:26).

So we are conquerors in this fight against sin, or at least we should be. No one in the world can accuse us when the Judge of all is on our side. Human courts and authorities can cause us trouble, but their judgments are not the ones that count. God has already arranged for us to be transformed into the same kind of resurrection body that Jesus already has. This is the original meaning of Romans 8:29, that we are predestined to be "conformed to the likeness of his Son." Paul's emphasis was not on determinism, on predestination for salvation. His emphasis was on what God has in store for us because he knew us ahead of time.

Paul was also not discussing the question of whether we can mess up what God has in store. When Paul said that nothing can separate us from the love of Christ, the context was clearly the "present sufferings" he had been talking about (8:18). No external force "in all creation" has any power to dislodge us from the destiny in the kingdom toward which God is leading us (8:39).

Paul linked the redemption of the enslaved creation to the redemption of bodies that will take place for those who are alive and remain at Christ's return (8:22–23). The created realm came under the power of sin when Adam sinned. Therefore, it seems likely that Paul saw eternity and the kingdom of God taking place on a redeemed, transformed earth rather than in heaven.

FOR FURTHER REFLECTION

1. If God is interested in redeeming the creation, does this fact have any implications for our attitude toward the world today? Should we worry about polluting the earth or replacing its beauty with the works of our hands, or would it honor God to value the earth and retain some of its natural beauty? Do you think God cares about what we do with his world?

2. Paul did not see sin as a normal part of Christian life, and Romans 7 is not about the struggle Paul was having with sin. Do you agree? Why or why not?

3. Why do you think Christians find it so easy to relate to Paul's image of the person struggling with sin? How does this chapter help you to understand the victory over sin that God can help us to experience?

6

ALL PART OF THE PLAN

GOD'S THE BOSS

Certain passages in the Bible are what I like to call "naughty verses." They are verses we find difficult to fit into our general understanding, verses that seem to say things that are contrary to what we expect the Bible to say. Romans 9 is one such naughty passage for me. In Romans 9:22, for example, Paul spoke of certain people who God had "prepared for destruction." Verse 18 also seems to say that God "hardens" certain people to make sure they do not receive his mercy.

In short, some of the verses in Romans 9 appear on the surface to say that God made certain people for the purpose of destroying them, similar to skeet shooting. He made them bad so that he could show his glory by blowing them to bits.

Some Christians, for whatever reason, are strangely drawn to this image of God. They make Romans 9 the basis of their thinking about God. They teach double predestination, the idea that God not only predetermines who will come to him and be saved, but also who will not come and be damned.

This view of God is difficult to reconcile with any meaningful sense of the idea that God is love. Instead, it teaches that God is nice to a select few that he has chosen according to his fancy. In what meaningful sense, though, does such a God love those whom he has not chosen for salvation, but instead has chosen for damnation? To most people, this looks more like evil than love.

Others take a similar view that God only chooses who will be saved, not who will be condemned. For example, John Calvin did not believe God chose for anyone to be damned; instead, everyone was already damned because of the sin of Adam. God thus shows mercy by choosing to save some who are already condemned, while leaving others in their condemned state.

We can at least appreciate Calvin's belief that God would not arbitrarily consign us to damnation. He must have sensed the difficulty in reconciling any normal definition of love with the idea that God would create some people just to show his glory in destroying them. Yet those who believe in double predestination are also being more consistent in their interpretation of Paul's language in Romans 9. Paul pictured the damned complaining to God (9:19–21).

The key to understanding Romans 9–11 is threefold. First, we need to understand the role these verses play in the overall thought of Romans. In particular, Paul was not really discussing our individual fates. He was trying to answer the question of why so many Gentiles had believed in Jesus and most Jews had not. Second, we need to realize that fatalism and determinism were key features of the world in which Paul lived. In that sense, there was a cultural dimension to his arguments here. Finally, the language game of predestination did not function primarily on a literal level. It served two basic purposes: first, to affirm that God is in control, and second, to assure the elect of God's favor toward them. Paul never used the language of predestination to deny salvation to anyone or to assure believers of their salvation regardless of what they did.

Romans 9–11 deals with the question of why so many Gentiles had come to believe in Christ when God's people themselves, the Jews, by and large, had not. In the traditional Reformation interpretation of Romans—that it was about how to get to heaven—these chapters seemed completely out of place. It has even been suggested that these chapters do not belong here, that they have been spliced into Romans at an arbitrary place.

But if you have been following the argument through the last few chapters of this book, you can begin to see that they are completely appropriate here. Romans 1–4 deals broadly with the fact that Jews, just like Gentiles, were sinners and violators of the law. All have sinned, Paul said (3:23), both Jew and Gentile. Thus, Jews needed Christ's atonement just as Gentiles did. Romans 6–9 deals broadly with the question of the Jewish Law. What was the purpose of the law if keeping it did not make a person right with God?

Questions like, "Why has Israel not believed?" or "Has God abandoned his people?" fit perfectly with what Paul had discussed thus far in the letter. In Romans 9, Paul's answer essentially was, "Who are you to question God? God is God and he can do whatever he wants" (see 9:20). Paul went on to answer these questions for his believing audience, so he apparently did not have a serious problem with them being asked. He rejected the protests of unbelieving Jews and Judaizing Christians who said Gentiles had to convert to Judaism to be saved.

His answer to those opponents was that God decides on whom he will or will not show mercy. Another important piece of the puzzle is that Paul was not primarily talking about individuals. His logic, especially if taken completely literally, had implications for individuals, but he was not advocating individual predestination. Instead, he was discussing God's right to have mercy on the Gentiles if he wanted to do so.

"For not all who are descended from Israel are Israel," Paul said (9:6). It was those who believed, those who pursued a right standing with God through their trust in Christ (9:30–32). It was only a portion of Israel, a "remnant," that was truly Israel (9:27). Paul said later that while God had removed some of the natural branches, he had also grafted in some Gentile branches (11:17).

Paul pushed back strongly on anyone who questioned God's judgment in doing such things. "Who are you, O man, to talk back to God? Shall what is formed say to him who formed it, 'Why did you make me like this?'" (9:20). Clay does not have the right to complain about the way the potter has made it, and if God wants to make some pottery for noble purposes and other for skeet shooting, that is his right as God (9:21–22).

Certainly it is. But it is essential to recognize that Paul was making an extreme point. The tone reminds me of things some parents say to their children when they are acting up: "If you don't stop, I'm going to pull this car over and make you walk!" "I'll get rid of that TV if you don't turn it off!" "I brought you into this world, and I can take you out!" They are extreme statements that, thankfully, the vast majority of parents do not mean to be understood literally. If they followed through with them, they would go to jail.[1]

God is certainly in charge; he is certainly the boss. I personally believe that God could command us to sacrifice our children if he wanted to (see Gen. 22). The sovereignty of God, his absolute authority, is a key Christian belief. It is also a key Christian belief that God does not act on his freedom in certain ways because of who he is. This is the heart of the predestination and free will debate: The logic of Romans 9 seems to conflict with the central Christian belief that God is love, the way Paul actually conducted his mission, and other things the New Testament says. The intent of this chapter is to sort out these tensions as best we can.

The issue is the question of God's sovereignty, his authority over everything. Friedrich Nietzsche, the famous skeptic of the late 1800s, said he came to the conclusion that if we are to thank God for the good things that happen to us, we have to give him credit for the bad as well.[2] Coming to this conclusion was part of the unraveling of his faith.

But his idea was not new. This is the standard view, for example, of the bulk of the Old Testament: "The LORD gave and the LORD has taken away; may the name of the LORD be praised" (Job 1:21). Similarly, some Christian traditions, like the Calvinist one, tend to see God orchestrating even the details of our lives. The popular Christian book, *The Purpose Driven Life*, presented a view of life that saw God's hand in almost everything that happens to you, with God teaching you lessons and helping you grow in almost every detail.[3]

However, as someone from the Wesleyan tradition, I do not accept this view. For one thing, there are passages in Scripture like James 1:13, which says no one should think that God tempts them to do wrong: "For God cannot be tempted by evil, nor does he tempt anyone." This verse gets at the heart of Nietzsche's complaint. If God is truly in control of the world, then he must also have control of the evil that happens in the world.

But there is a difference between God's directive will and his permissive will, between directly causing things to happen and merely allowing them to happen. God is sovereign, and that means he is ultimately in control of everything. The question is whether he micro-manages everything directly or gives a degree of freedom.

Some scholars argue that if God allowed someone to disagree with him or violate his will, then he would not truly be sovereign. But this argument seems rather unsophisticated. Could not a parent intentionally allow a child to experience the consequences of disobedience so that the child can learn and grow from it? This seems like a more mature, sophisticated picture of God than one that is in a rage every time someone disobeys him, or worse, causes people to disobey so he can show his greatness by blasting them out of existence. God is secure enough in his sovereignty to allow people to disagree with him.

This is the position I take and will advocate for in the rest of this chapter. Romans 9 has some naughty verses for this point of view, but every theological opinion has passages that create difficulty. The Calvinist view, by contrast, seems to create a picture of God that at best has him arbitrarily deciding who he will save and at worst has him create some people in order to destroy. This does not fit with the picture of God elsewhere and seems to take this language game of Paul too literally.

For God to be sovereign, he must, in a sense, "sign off" on everything that happens. But it does not mean he must directly orchestrate and plan everything that happens. The best answer to the problem of evil, although it is not perfect, is that a world in which God gives people the freedom to make good and bad moral choices is a better world than one in which they cannot help but do good. God thus has created a world where people can disobey him for a greater good—and a world where we find evil and pain. And it is a world where we can choose to serve God, and thus a world with great potential for authentic rather than forced good.

THE DESTINY OF ISRAEL

So Romans 9–11 is not primarily about whether God determines who will be saved and who will be damned. Individual predestination is a related issue, but it also relates to what Paul really addressed in these chapters, which is the fate of Israel. It must have seemed peculiar that more Gentiles than Jews would believe that Jesus was king. One of the purposes of Romans 9–11 was to explain this strange phenomenon. Paul's answer, in the end, was the mystery of God's will. If this is how God wants it, then that is his business, and you had better not question him about it!

Even here, to get the full picture of what Paul really thought, we cannot simply stop with Romans 9. Unless we read on to Romans 11, we end up with a skewed sense of Paul's view toward Israel. For example, one perspective sometimes taught today is called "replacement theology." It is the idea that the church has now completely replaced Israel within God's plan. This view uses Romans 9:6 as its fundamental verse: "For not all who are descended from Israel are Israel." Such individuals see the church as the true Israel; only ethnic Jews who believe, along with Gentiles who believe are part of true Israel. They do not see any place in God's plan for the nation of Israel or non-believing Jews today.

This perspective likely contains some truth, but it is not the whole truth. To arrive at this view, you have to isolate and lift out Romans 9:6 from Paul's broader discussion. Romans 11 makes it clear that Paul saw the dominance of Gentile Christianity as a temporary thing and ethnic Israel would eventually believe in Jesus. It has not happened yet, and Paul himself might have been surprised that God allowed Israel to be destroyed and virtually nonexistent for almost two thousand years. But we cannot let these complications stand in the way of listening to what Paul said and meant.

Paul asked, "Did God reject his people?" (Rom. 11:1). The answer: "By no means!" (11:1). Paul himself was an Israelite, so God obviously had not rejected all of Israel. As in the days of Elijah, God had chosen a "remnant" in his graciousness. Thus far, Paul's argument was similar to what he said in Romans 9. God gave the unbelieving in Israel a "sluggish spirit" so that they would not see or hear the message (11:8 NRSV). "May their eyes be darkened so they cannot see" (11:10).

However, Paul then continued: "Did they stumble so as to fall beyond recovery?" (11:11). Here is the key to understanding Paul's perspective on Israel. Even those "predestined for disbelief" could come back! This was certainly not the kind of predestination taught in some Christian traditions. Indeed, John Calvin reasoned that if God decided a person was saved, the person must remain saved until the end. God does not change his mind; he has made the decision from all eternity, and our will has no part in it.

In Calvin's thinking, the predestined cannot change places.[4] Either God chose you or he did not. But in the rest of Romans 11, Paul charted out the eventual return of ethnic Israel from its hardness of heart. God had a plan, Paul said, to bring the Gentiles to salvation, and Israel's hardness was part of the plan. First, God would use their hard hearts to bring the Gentiles in. Then, he would bring the Jews back in again too.

Paul was trying to make sense of a troubling phenomenon among the earliest Christians: Gentiles were more receptive to the Christian message than Jews were. Paul explained it by recourse to the mystery of God's will. But this was all part of God's plan. If you think of God's people as a tree, God had cut out a good number of the natural (Jew) branches and grafted in some Gentile branches that were not part of the original tree (11:17). This made the natural branches jealous (11:11).

This privilege was not a matter for boasting, as if the Gentile branches were eternally secure. If God did not spare the natural branches, he certainly would not spare the grafted ones if they became arrogant about their new identity (11:21). These are not the sorts of things you would expect Paul to say if the Calvinist interpretation of Romans 9 is correct. The destiny of each type of branch was reversible. Indeed, the way the branches conducted themselves had a direct bearing on whether they were allowed to stay in the tree.

In short, Paul saw our presence in the tree as contingent on our human response. Most of ethnic Israel was out because of unbelief (11:20). But they could come back if they believed. Many Gentiles were in because they believed, but if they became arrogant, they would be removed. Since these possibilities contradict the Calvinist doctrine of predestination, Paul's language of election must function differently than predestinarians believe.

So God's plan, Paul said, was for Israel to reject Jesus as Messiah, which in some way facilitated the Gentile mission in Paul's mind. Paul also saw the acceptance of the gospel by Gentiles as making his own people jealous. He did not spell out exactly what he meant, but he apparently believed it would somehow eventually lead ethnic Israel back to God and belief in Jesus as Messiah.

His argument reached its climax in 11:25–32. Part of Israel was experiencing a hardening (11:25). There is no real ambiguity about who Paul had in mind here. He was talking about the "hardened" part of Israel, those ethnic Jews who did not believe in Jesus. He was talking about the natural branches, the unbelieving Jews, whom God had removed. The purpose, as he has said, was so that the "full number" of the Gentiles could come in (11:25).

But then, Paul said, "all Israel will be saved" (11:26). Paul's statement may be difficult for us to process, but it is not ambiguous. He contrasted the part with the whole. The part was hardened, but all would be saved. Some scholars have thought that Paul must have meant that all *true* Israel would be saved, hearkening back to 9:6. Not only would such a meaning be pointless—to say "all the saved will be saved"—but it also ignores the clear train of thought in the passage: right now, part is out; then, all will be in.

Christ will thus take away the sins of Israel (11:27). He will "turn godlessness away from Jacob" (11:26). Paul did not explain the timing in relation to Christ, although clearly Israel's salvation was still future. He said that "the deliverer will come from Zion," referring to Jesus (11:26). But was he talking about Jesus coming out of Zion in the future or about Jesus' previous coming out of Zion?[5] Was Paul saying Israel will believe around the time of Jesus' return from heaven, perhaps in preparation for or as a consequence of his return? Or was he simply quoting a passage that indicated the Jews would believe in their messiah as a consequence of Jesus coming to earth?

Either way, Paul clearly pointed to the eventual salvation of Israel. They were, at the time, God's enemies because of what he was doing with the Gentiles (11:28). But they were still the elect of God, the chosen ones: "God's gifts and his call are irrevocable" (11:29), meaning that God will never turn his back on Israel. He might destroy a generation, but he will not break his word to Abraham. The Gentiles have received mercy because of Israel's disobedience (11:30), but eventually Israel will also receive mercy because of what God is doing with the Gentiles (11:31), and God will then have mercy on everyone (11:32).

LIFE REFLECTIONS

In the end, it does not seem difficult to see what Paul was saying in these verses. What is difficult is to know what to do with them today. For some Christians, it seems obvious. They believe Paul's prediction related directly to the reestablishment of Israel as a political nation in 1948. Many American Christians believe the United States must support Israel politically against her enemies as the biblical, Christian thing to do. This perspective was a powerful force behind the reformation of Israel in 1948 in the first place.

Many Christians today send money to Israel and consider opposition to Palestinian causes a Christian duty. Visits to the Holy Land are the regular fare of American churches and such Christians often identify closely with Israel. A theme park in Orlando, Florida, has even recreated Jerusalem and its temple from the time of Christ for Christians to experience (the Holy Land Experience). Meanwhile, the dispensationalist understanding of the Bible looks to a time when the temple will be rebuilt and its sacrifices resumed.[6] Occasionally you hear a rumor that some group of Jews have made all the tools and implements of the temple and have them ready to go as soon as Israel recovers the Temple Mount from the Muslims.

We will know what God has in store only when it happens. Far be it from me to say that the restoration of Israel as a nation might not be part of some plan God has for the end of this age. However, we should keep a number of cautions and clarifications in mind.

First, Paul knew nothing of the destruction of Jerusalem or its temple that took place in A.D. 70. Even 2 Thessalonians 2 said nothing about a man of lawlessness setting himself up in a rebuilt temple. It seems to be referring to the temple that was standing at the time. One of the reasons some people like the idea that the church has replaced Israel is because the Israel Paul probably had in mind has been gone for over nineteen hundred years.

Second, the political Israel that currently exists is not the Israel of promise—at least not yet. Romans 11:26 says, "All Israel will be saved," implying that the part of Israel that did not believe then would come to believe later.[7] But those who live in the nation of Israel are not Christians. Indeed, the majority of them are secular Jews who do not believe in God at all. And it is actually illegal to try to convert someone to Christianity in Israel.

This is a very important point. From Paul's perspective, those in Israel today are still unbelieving Israel. From the perspective of the Gospels, those in Israel today are still those whose rejection of Christ led to the destruction of Jerusalem. Certainly we must be very careful here. You will not find any basis for anti-Semitism, crusades, or holocausts here. Neither will you find any justification for giving political Israel any special favors in the way it behaves as a nation. The nations of the world must act even-handedly with Israel as with all other nations and friends.

Another point of insight is to realize that, at least up until recent times, far more Palestinians have been Christians, at least in name, than Israelis have. Even though the city of Nazareth is in Israel, it is overwhelmingly populated by Christian Palestinians. The city of Bethlehem is in Palestinian territory, but up until the last few years, its population was predominantly Christian. Many American Christians have blindly supported non-believing Israel over believers among the Palestinians.

What then do we do with Romans 11:26? I would not be surprised if this verse played out in a way that would have surprised Paul. Predictions in Scripture are often fulfilled in some segmented or spiritualized way. For example, Daniel 11 reads for the most part as a symbolic presentation of events that took place around the time of the Maccabean revolt from 167–164 B.C. Then suddenly at 12:1, we find verses that best relate to the resurrection at the time of Christ's return, which is yet to come.

Matthew 24 similarly discusses events relating to the destruction of Jerusalem in A.D. 70. Then suddenly in 24:29, the prediction also jumps to Christ's return, which has not yet occurred. So it is at least possible to read Romans 11:26 the same way. Paul did not foresee the amount of time that would pass between his day and Israel's turning to faith in Jesus as Messiah.

While it fits the spirit of the Bible for Israel to have a future in God's plan, some elements in God's plan are adjustable. There is an example of God changing his plan in Jonah, where God did not destroy the city of Nineveh because of the people's repentance. In other words, God can alter his plan because of human response.[8] The proper conclusion seems to be that God's prophecies of judgment and salvation are adjustable and contingent on human response.

The New Testament writers also sometimes took Old Testament verses figuratively or in secondary senses. Deuteronomy 25:4 originally told farmers not to muzzle their oxen when they were treading grain, but Paul took this verse to foreshadow the need for churches to support their ministers materially (1 Cor. 9:9–11). The original audience of Isaiah 7:14 would not have on that basis predicted a messiah to be born of a virgin seven hundred years later. The sign in question was originally to king Ahaz about a child who had already been born.[9] To interpret it as referring to Jesus is to read it figuratively or spiritually.

Ezekiel 40–43 is another example. Ezekiel prophesied during the exile of Israel (586–538 B.C.) and predicted that a glorious temple would eventually be rebuilt and that God's glory would one day return to it (43:5). The temple was indeed rebuilt, which is a significant problem with modern teaching about prophecy that expects the temple to be rebuilt again. All the predictions of the temple's rebuilding were made prior to its rebuilding in 538 B.C.

The problem was that the temple was not rebuilt with the grandeur Ezekiel pictured. And we cannot take Ezekiel's temple literally in reference to any temple yet to be rebuilt, because God's glory will never again fill an earthly temple. The New Testament book of Hebrews makes it quite clear that the true sanctuary of God is in heaven and is not built by human hands (Heb. 9:24). The New Jerusalem in Revelation 21:2 does not have a temple. So we must interpret this passage in Ezekiel spiritually—either God changed his mind because of Israel's response to him or he was speaking symbolically in some way.

The bottom line in much of this discussion is that we will know what God had in mind most clearly after it happens, and we must look for justice in Israel as God looks for justice in his church. We should not live our lives or shape our foreign policy as a nation around a questionable interpretation of passages like Romans 11:26. The course of the future has always been vague looking forward and only clear looking backward. Our task is to be faithful and to call others to faithfulness.

FOR FURTHER REFLECTION

1. Do you agree that Romans 9–11 is really about Israel and the Gentiles, rather than about individual destinies? Why or why not?

2. This chapter was the beginning of us wrestling with the question of predestination, a topic we will continue to think about in the next chapter. At this point in the discussion, what solution would you offer to the puzzle of fitting predestination with human response? Does the Calvinist answer undermine any meaningful understanding of God as love? Does the Arminian answer do justice to the biblical texts? To God's sovereignty? Can we accept both principles and resort to mystery—that the workings of God are beyond comprehension?

3. What would you say is the most appropriate attitude of Christians today toward Israel as a nation: (1) give them our unconditional support; (2) honor them because of Abraham, the prophets, Jesus, and the apostles, but expect the same righteousness we expect of other nations; or (3) treat them the same as any other nation?

7

HOW TO BE SAVED

THE ROMANS ROAD IN CONTEXT

Enveloped within Paul's thoughts about God's plan for the Gentiles are some familiar verses. We have heard them described in terms of "getting saved," "becoming a Christian," or "getting to heaven." For example, Romans 10:13 says, "Everyone who calls on the name of the Lord will be saved," quoting Joel 2:32. Romans 10:9 features in the "Roman Road," a series of verses from Romans meant to lead a person through the logic of becoming a Christian. On the Romans Road, Romans 3:23 first tells us that "all have sinned," which of course includes you and me. Then Romans 6:23 tells us that the "wages" for our sin is death. But Romans 5:8 gives us hope: "While we were still sinners, Christ died for us." Finally, we come to Romans 10:9: "If you confess with your mouth, 'Jesus is Lord,' and believe in your heart that God raised him from the dead, you will be saved."

Hopefully the last few chapters have made it clear that, while this way of using these verses is not wrong, it approaches them differently than Paul did. For Paul, all these statements had to do with the question of whether Gentiles could escape God's coming judgment. This is what being saved and salvation meant for Paul. It referred to escaping God's wrathful judgment on the day when Christ returns and everyone gives him an account for the deeds they have done on earth (including believers; see 2 Cor. 5:10). In that sense, no one is *literally* saved yet because salvation is yet to come on the day of judgment.[1] When we speak of "getting saved," we are really speaking of our assurance of something that has not yet happened.

So in Paul's mind, the *all* in "all have sinned" meant both Jew and Gentile rather than only Gentiles—all, or both, have sinned. And Paul situated his arguments about the wages of sin and Christ dying for the ungodly in a story where the Jewish Law set the standard for sin and where Israel would eventually recognize that Jesus was its Messiah. Later Christian theology has universalized Paul's thinking in ways that are not wrong, but are slightly out of context. The law became the universal moral law rather than the Jewish Law. The *all* in "all have sinned" shifted to the individual trying to be justified and ultimately saved, rather than Gentiles as well as Jews.

So Romans 10:9 is situated in a passage where Paul was asking why so many Gentiles were headed for salvation while most Jews were not. Paul said the reason was that they insisted on doing it their way rather than God's way. God's way was to make the world right with him through trust in Jesus, but many Jews wanted to be right with God through keeping the Jewish Law (Rom. 9:30–33). They stumbled over God's plan for righteousness, a right standing before God, through

Jesus (9:33). They tried to establish a right standing before God on their own, rather than by following what God had in mind (10:3).[2]

Christ is thus the goal of the law, that to which the Jewish Law points (10:4). Some traditions take the phrase "Christ is the end of the law" to mean that Christ brings an end to the law. But it is far more likely that Paul was saying Christ is the goal, the *telos* of the law. As Paul said in Galatians 3:24, "the law was our guardian" (NLT), a "tutor to lead us to Christ" (NASB). But since Christ had come, born under the law to redeem Jews under the law (4:4–5), faith had also come, and neither Jews nor Gentiles needed the tutor any more (3:25). We have grown in the maturity of salvation history now to have the status of sons and daughters who no longer need the law as our guardian.

So what is God's plan for right standing? It is to trust in what God has done through Jesus the Christ. Paul's letter to the Romans had already set out the plan. First, "God demonstrates his own love for us in this: While we were still sinners, Christ died for us" (Rom. 5:8). Paul never really spelled out the specifics of how Christ's death worked. When he said that "Christ died for our sins according to the Scriptures" (1 Cor. 15:3), Paul was not laying out a specific doctrine about Christ taking our place. The word *for* simply meant he died to deal with them. Paul did not say exactly how.

One picture he gave us was the transference of the curse of our sin to Christ on the cross: "Christ redeemed us from the curse of the law by becoming a curse for us, for it is written: 'Cursed is everyone who is hung on a tree'" (Gal. 3:13).[3] Paul seemed to imply in 1 Corinthians 1:23 that the cross stood at the center of his preaching, which makes the logic of Galatians 3:13 a significant key to understanding Paul's thinking. In this picture of the cross, Christ did not take our punishment; he took our curse. Like the scapegoat of Leviticus 16, our defilement (not our debt or punishment) was transferred to Christ.

We also find the picture of Jesus' death as a sacrifice here and there in Paul's writings. The most explicit is in Romans 3:25, "Through his faithfulness, God displayed Jesus as the place of sacrifice where mercy is found by means of his blood" (CEB). This translation is debated, with the NIV and NRSV going with the more common "sacrifice of atonement." The reason the CEB translates it as "place of atonement" is because the word Paul regularly used referred to the cover of the ark of the covenant in the Old Testament, the place where blood was taken once a year by the high priest to atone for the sins of Israel (see Lev. 16:14). One way or another, Paul was thinking of Jesus' death in sacrificial terms.

Atonement is reconciliation by way of an offering. The idea of Jesus' death as such an offering appears throughout Paul's letters. Romans 8:3, for example, likely speaks of God sending Jesus as a sin offering. First Corinthians 5:7 refers to Christ as a Passover lamb, sacrificed for believers. The inner dynamics of sacrifice are often difficult for us to understand. Sacrifice fits roughly in the category of "satisfaction" theories of atonement, where Christ's death satisfies the wrath of God or propitiates it. But it is not clear that Paul connected the dots in this way. In some ways, C. S. Lewis' picture of a "deep magic" that is mysterious and inexplicable may come closer to Paul's meaning—a less defined sense that the order of things was restored through the offering of blood.[4]

Jesus' resurrection from the dead was also significant for Paul in getting us right with God. "If Christ has not been raised," Paul wrote, "you are still in your sins" (1 Cor. 15:17). In Romans 4:25, Paul said that Christ was "raised to life for our justification." Perhaps hidden within such statements was yet another Christian theory of atonement, namely, the *Christus Victor* or "Christ the conqueror" view.[5] Paul spoke of death as the last enemy for Christ to defeat, one that he will definitively defeat at the time of the final resurrection (1 Cor. 15:20–28).

Again, it is difficult for us to discern what Paul was thinking. After all, Paul did not think of death or sin as a person. It is mysterious to us exactly how Jesus' victorious resurrection might defeat sin and death. Indeed, just because Paul found such language natural does not necessarily mean that he could explain the specifics of how it worked either. Nevertheless, "the sting of death is sin" (1 Cor. 15:56) and "the law of the Spirit of life in Christ Jesus has set you free from the law of sin and of death" (Rom. 8:2 NRSV). Somehow, Christ's resurrection entailed the defeat of these forces against us.

LIFE REFLECTIONS ON THE ROMANS ROAD

The Christian really does not need to know all the ins and outs of how atonement works. We know we are separated from God. We know that God sent Christ to reconcile us to him. Did it work because our curse was transferred to Jesus? Did it work because Jesus absorbed God's wrath? Did it work because by raising Christ God defeated the powers of sin and death? Paul used all these pictures. And while we may not fully comprehend the details, we know it worked.

But how does a person appropriate Christ's death? Romans 10:9 says, "That if you confess with your mouth, 'Jesus is Lord,' and believe in your heart that God raised him from the dead, you will be saved." The verses immediately before seem to emphasize how easy a thing this confession is. You do not have to ascend to heaven to bring Christ down or descend into the abyss to bring him up (10:6–7). You can make such a confession wherever you are (10:8).

The confession, "Jesus is Lord," seems to have been a key part of becoming a Jesus follower in the early church. It may even have been part of early baptismal rituals. No one, Paul said, can truly make this confession unless the Spirit of God enables them (1 Cor. 12:3). It is this confession that every tongue will make at the final judgment (Phil. 2:11).

To confess the lordship of Jesus is to believe that God raised him from the dead (Rom. 10:9). Indeed, Paul associated Jesus' lordship with the kingship that Christ assumed after his resurrection, just as Paul saw Jesus being enthroned as Son of God at that time (see 1:3). The Philippian hymn has the same timing: God's exaltation of Jesus after his death on the cross led to the confession, "Jesus Christ is Lord" by all creatures (Phil. 2:8–11). The books of Acts and Hebrews present Jesus' lordship in the same way (see Acts 2:34–36; 13:33; Heb. 1:4–5).

As easy as it might seem to confess Jesus as Lord, confessing someone as Lord is serious business. We do not have much experience these days in what it is like to serve a king. We can be sure that it requires complete obedience and willingness to do the king's will. As much as Paul emphasized God's graciousness and mercy, he left no room for those who persisted in certain behaviors to be part of the kingdom of God, whether they were part of the church or not (see 1 Cor. 6:9–10).

But how does God change us? We caught a glimpse in the last chapter of how Paul saw the Spirit empowering us over sin. Paul also spoke frequently of our being "in Christ." In Romans 6:4, Paul pictured us being buried with Christ through our baptism. We are united with him in his death and thus united with him in his resurrection (6:5). We are crucified with Christ—our old self dies (Rom. 6:6; Gal. 2:20)— and now Christ lives in us. The life we now live we live in Christ's faithfulness (Gal. 2:20).[6]

So everyone who calls on the name of the Lord will be saved from God's coming wrath on the day of judgment (Rom. 10:13). For Paul, the Gentiles were the key part of the "all" that some of his fellow believers were not including. But neither would the Jews be saved if they did not demonstrate faith in Jesus as Lord, no matter how well they kept the finer points of the Jewish Law. Paul's mission was to take the good news of faith to the Gentiles. After all, how could they confess faith in Jesus if they never heard the good news (10:14)? And to hear the good news required a preacher. Paul was that preacher, and he hoped that the Romans would participate in his ongoing "sending" to the ends of the earth (10:15).

PAUL'S LANGUAGE OF ELECTION

Paul regularly used language of predestination and election. It was clearly a major category of his thinking and language, but what did he mean by it? I started the last chapter with the claim that such language served two basic purposes. It affirmed that God is in control and nothing happens without his approval. And yet, it would clearly go against the tenor of Paul and Scripture as a whole to suggest that God caused Peter to be a hypocrite at Antioch or directly commanded Satan to tempt Jesus. The biblical texts do not say or imply such things.

At least as important as what Paul said with his words is what he did with them. Paul's words were not propositions in a philosophy textbook; they were real-life statements with common sense limits, often accompanied by emotion, and usually formulated in such a way as to persuade. Later thinkers like Augustine or Calvin then tried to fill in the blanks and connect the dots, as we all do when we reflect on such things. The problem is that when we connect the dots, we end up with ideas that do not fit with other things Paul said.

Paul never used predestination language in a way that ensured an individual's future without condition. For example, Paul must have considered himself to be one of the elect. Surely he considered himself to be justified by faith. He had more confidence of his own place among the sanctified than he did the bulk of the Corinthian church. Yet he still expressed the possibility that he would not make it. He disciplined his life so that after running so well in the race of faith, he would not end up disqualified for the prize of salvation (1 Cor. 9:27). He continued on his course of suffering, saying, "if somehow I may attain the resurrection from the dead" (Phil. 3:11 NRSV). A predestinarian can certainly explain such verses: Even though Paul was unsure of his election, God was certain of it. But this explanation is imposed on the text, not something Paul said.

Similarly, Paul did not use predestination language in a way that ensured that someone "prepared for destruction" would inevitably be damned (Rom. 9:22). After speaking in the strongest terms about God's sovereign right to predestine the disbelieving in Israel for destruction, Paul then went on in Romans 11:23 to say that those who had been removed could be grafted back in. In other words, he did not talk about predestination as if what was predetermined is unconditionally predetermined. Again, the predestinarian can try to explain away what Paul said elsewhere. If we could see behind the curtain, they might say, we would see that God predestined this individual Israelite first to be removed and then to be grafted back in. But that is not what Paul actually said.

In the end, Paul's predestination language functioned as "after the fact" language. It primarily served to affirm those who had responded to the gospel with faith. And it functioned in this way primarily on a corporate rather than individual level. It functioned to assure the "elect" of God's favor toward them without guaranteeing that favor apart from their continued faithfulness. It functioned in his rhetoric more on an effective and cohesive level than on a propositional level. Meanwhile, he hardly ever used such language in relation to the wicked. He did so in Romans 9 in a context of highly charged rhetoric in relation to God's right to do whatever he wants with his creation.

So we return to some of the insights we had at the beginning of the chapter. Paul's language of predestination fit well with the fatalism of his world. Also like the fatalism of his world, Paul did not speak of election in a way that was mutually exclusive with freedom of choice. Rather, we know what God has willed by what happens, after the fact. Predestination language, while sounding predictive, actually functions entirely in retrospect. It does not impact who can be saved or how one is to go about mission.

LIFE REFLECTIONS ON ELECTION

So when we get to application, we can see that no matter what we believe in theory about predestination, we must all live as if we have free will. We must live as if the way we live out our faithfulness to God matters. We must live as if we can lose our right standing with God. We must conduct the mission of the church as if everyone can be saved. We must do all these things in faith that God is in control and that nothing happens without his approval. Who knows? Perhaps in some way that would blow our minds, God, who is beyond our understanding, was able to create a world in which he both determines everything and gives us the ability to choose or not choose him.

Romans 8:28–30 says, "We know that God works all things together for good for the ones who love God, for those who are called according to his purpose. We know this because God knew them in advance, and he decided in advance that they would be conformed to the image of his Son. That way his Son would be the first of many brothers and sisters. Those who God decided in advance would be conformed to his Son, he also called. Those whom he called, he also made righteous. Those whom he made righteous, he also glorified" (CEB).

Christians regularly invoke Romans 8:28 with the sense that no matter what difficult circumstance you might be in, God will work it out for your good. Certainly God always has our good in mind and helps us in all our trials and troubles. But in context, we can see that the good in view goes far beyond our immediate circumstances to eternity, indeed beyond us as individuals to all believers as a whole. The good here is to be conformed to the image of God's Son. What did Paul mean? He said that we will bear the likeness of Jesus in the resurrection (1 Cor. 15:49), that our bodies will be transformed to be like Jesus' glorious body (Phil. 3:21). He spoke of Christ as the firstfruits of the dead, with us following him (1 Cor. 15:20; see also Heb. 2:10). In short, the good that God is working out almost certainly refers to our glorification that will take place at the resurrection.[7]

God has already decided that we will experience this transformation together, that our bodies will all be conformed to the form of his glorified body. Knowing who would participate in the resurrection, he called us; he elected us. He planned for us to become right with God, to be justified. He planned for us to be glorified in the resurrection, just as Christ was.

FOR FURTHER REFLECTION

1. Have you been convinced that predestination language is, more than anything else, after-the-fact language that affirms those who have believed and affirms that God is in control without really connecting the dots the way Calvin did? Why or why not?

2. Let's revisit a question we asked at the end of the previous chapter. After this further reading, what solution would you now offer to the puzzle of fitting predestination with human response? Does the Calvinist answer undermine any meaningful understanding of God as love? Does the Arminian answer do justice to the biblical texts? What about to God's sovereignty? Can we accept both principles and resort to mystery—that the workings of God are beyond comprehension?

3. Summarize how a person becomes saved in a simple enough way that you could present it to someone who had never heard about Christianity.

GETTING ALONG TOGETHER

TRANSFORMED MINDS

In the first eleven chapters of Romans, Paul explained his understanding of God's righteousness: God's recurring action to save his people and the world. Paul presented the problem of sin and judgment that both Jews and Gentiles shared in common. He rejoiced in the salvation God made possible through Christ. He reflected on the purpose of the Jewish Law in God's plan and clarified that he did not see God's grace as an excuse to sin. Finally, he reflected on why Israel largely rejected its own Messiah, while the Gentiles, in significant numbers, mysteriously believed in Christ.

That whole argument led to the huge "therefore" of Romans 12:1. If all the arguments Paul had presented were true, then the Romans should have done all the things he was about to say. First, they should have presented their bodies as living sacrifices to God (12:1), and second, their minds were to be transformed so that they understood what God's will was, rather than thinking in the terms of this world (12:2). The first half of Romans is more theological; the second half is more practical. Paul's teaching on how to live in chapters 12–15 played out in concrete, specific terms what it means to have a transformed mind and what it means to sacrifice your body to God.

The idea of offering our bodies as sacrifices might sound familiar. Back in Romans 6, Paul told the Romans to offer the parts of their bodies not as instruments of wickedness but as "instruments of righteousness" (6:13). Our old self has been crucified with him (6:6). We have died to what once bound us (7:6). Our bodies are dead because of sin (8:10).

These images of death all relate to our former way of sinful living. We have died with Christ so that we may be raised to "newness of life" (6:4 NRSV). And though our bodies are dead because of sin, God gives life to our mortal bodies while we are still in this world through his Spirit dwelling inside us (8:11). To offer our bodies as living sacrifices, holy and acceptable to God (12:1), is to die to our sinful flesh and rise with Christ to a new life as we continue to live in this world. We should think of Paul's instructions in Romans 12–15 as some of the specifics of what that new living might look like.

Such newness of life involves a transformed way of thinking that is different from the way unbelievers think. For some, it is tempting to make Paul's words in Romans 12:2 into a command to study and get a set of ideas right. Socrates allegedly once said, "Right thinking leads to right action."[1] Some who give high priority to reason and thinking mistakenly take Paul to say that the key is to get our ideas and worldviews in order and that if we can only get our ideas right, then everything else will take care of itself. Our right ideas will play themselves out into right living.

Unfortunately, this is just not the case. Most people have significant points of discontinuity between their professed ideas and how they live. Some of us may be unaware of the discontinuity, but many realize it and still do not change their way of life. How many people make no attempt to stop smoking or control their eating even though they know it is extremely harmful to their bodies? How many people in the past have believed in God but continued to live in ways they believed were wrong?

Further, the ideas we profess often come from our understanding of life, rather than the other way around. The arguments we give are just as often meant to justify the conclusion we want to hold rather than honest attempts to be objective about the evidence. We humans are simply not rational creatures for the most part, and those interpreters of Romans 12:2 who see the verse in relation to reasoning things out logically are destined for never-ending frustration.

In the end, though, logic is not what Paul meant when he spoke of a transformed mind. The verses that follow make it clear that he had in mind a way of thinking about each other, or more precisely, our attitudes toward one another, as in Philippians 2. In the paragraph immediately following 12:1–2, Paul told the Romans not to have an inflated opinion of themselves, but to recognize that each one has a role to play in the body of Christ (12:3–8). In the rest of Romans 12, Paul gave some guidelines for loving relationships with others, including those who might mistreat us. All these instructions on Christian living are specific examples of the transformed and renewed mind Paul mentioned in 12:2.

TRANSFORMED COMMUNITIES

Paul went on to present how a transformed mind shows itself in a community of faith. We must understand our place in the church and not think of ourselves more highly than we ought. We each have a role to play. Some of us prophesy; some serve; some teach or encourage; others lead, show mercy, or give to the needs of others. As Paul earlier told the Corinthians (1 Cor. 12:12), together we make a single body, and all the parts play their particular roles (Rom. 12:4–5).

Paul did not intend to give an exhaustive or unchanging list. Indeed, each list in his body of writings was a little different (see 1 Cor. 12:4–11; Eph. 4:11). For example, when he addressed Corinth where the practice of tongues was causing conflict, he put tongues on the list. But in his letter to Rome where tongues presumably were not an issue, he did not include it. Indeed, we can imagine that his list in Romans gives us a much more typical picture of community functions.

Paul's goal was thus to merely give a taste of the different roles a person can play in the body of Christ and to affirm each individual as of equal value in God's eyes, even though they may be differently gifted by God. He was not setting up categories for some gift test you might take.[2] We should not think of ourselves as better than anyone else but be thankful that God has enabled us to make a contribution to others. These are, after all, gifts God has given us for which we cannot take credit. We did not earn them, and we cannot boast of having them.

We should not assume that the gifts Paul mentioned are completely distinct from each other, but they do seem to give us a snapshot of the early church. Paul mentioned prophesy first, and distinguished it from teaching and leading. In reality, the same individual might be gifted to do all three. Or maybe a person would not do them at the same time. Prophesy in Paul's churches was a charismatic activity where God revealed truths to the community through a person inspired in the moment (see 1 Cor. 14:24–25). The one who led was to do it with diligence, which was presumably a sign of someone gifted to lead.

Encouragement and showing mercy are harder to distinguish from each other, as is serving. Indeed, one can encourage with prophecy (1 Cor. 14:3). The word for *serving* is related to the word Paul used elsewhere of a deacon (see Phil. 1:1; Rom. 16:1), which apparently was an identifiable ministry role in at least some of his churches. Giving to those in need seems similar to serving in this way. The word for *encouragement* can also have a sense of admonition or charging others, which is a function prophecy can also serve. So these roles are more general than fixed or completely distinct.

It is when we get to Romans 13:8–10 that Paul summarized the bottom line of what it means to have a transformed and renewed mind. Like Jesus in Matthew 22:34–40, Paul summarized all of God's expectations not only for the Jews but for all humanity. People will follow the whole essence of the Jewish Law—not commit adultery, murder, steal, or covet—if they love their neighbor as themselves. "Love does no harm to its neighbor. Therefore love is the fulfillment of the law" (Rom. 13:10). Love of one's neighbor is truly the essence of what it means for our minds to be transformed and to not let sin reign in our mortal bodies.

Paul already gave some of the concrete specifics of such a loving mind in Romans 12. Love honors others above oneself, not merely with words but sincerety (12:9–10). It is not proud or conceited, and it is willing to associate with those on whom society looks with disdain, knowing that all it has is a gift from God (12:16).

Human nature is amazingly capable of getting around what it is supposed to do. Once we realize that we should not speak and act in ways that put us above others, we may then take pride in how much more humble we are than others. Although it is not as common to see such behavior these days, there was a time where humility could be a sort of game, where people wanted others to see how humble they were by not accepting compliments or praise. But true love acts like a brother or sister who has the best interests of others in mind (12:10).

Love shares with others among God's people who are in need (12:13). Love shows hospitality to those who have nowhere to stay and nothing to eat (12:13). Love rejoices with those who rejoice and mourns with those who mourn (12:15; see also 1 Cor. 13:4–6). Competitive human nature can easily do the opposite. It can be glad to get one up on the person who was set back or be annoyed at someone else who gets ahead. Love lives in harmony with others (Rom. 12:16).

A transformed mind does not enjoy evil and clings to what is good (12:9). One sign of an immature Christian mind is a certain fiendish enjoyment of the misfortunes of others or secret liking for things we know are unpleasing to God. A transformed mind is full of spiritual fervor and zeal to serve the Lord. But this is not zeal like the unbelieving Israel of Paul's day had, a zeal "not based on knowledge" (10:2). It is a zealous love rather than zeal to condemn and exclude, as Paul's opponents wished to exclude the Gentiles from salvation. The renewing of one's mind that takes place through the Spirit is a mind transformed to love one another.

THE STRONG AND THE WEAK

Although Paul had never been to Rome, he arguably knew a little about the church there.[3] In particular, Roman believers may have debated things like eating meat from pagan temples just like the Corinthians did. In Romans 14–15, Paul labeled the two sides in such issues as the strong and the weak. The strong were those whose faith was strong enough to eat meat that had been sacrificed to a pagan god or who could give every day to the Lord without doubt (14:1–2). The weak were those who were troubled about their meat being unclean or who felt obligated to observe the Jewish Sabbath (14:5).

To be sure, we should take into account the possibility that there was a significant amount of rhetoric here. Paul made the strong feel good by putting them in a position of knowledge and strength. But his goal was to lead them to respect and honor those who were more conservative. In a sense, he massaged the ego of the people who felt free to do certain things, while moving them toward being sensitive to those who did not.

His argument was very similar to what he said about "disputable matters" at Corinth, although it was more general here in Romans. Paul gave no evidence in this chapter that the debate was a Jew-Gentile issue at Rome. We will grow in our thinking about the early church if we recognize the strong likelihood that there were both Jews who were ultra-liberal on these issues and Gentiles who were ultra-conservative on them.

The issue of eating to which Paul alluded is almost certainly the same question he faced at Corinth—whether a believer should or should not eat meat that had been sacrificed to an idol. In fact, he was writing Romans from the city of Corinth, where that saga was no doubt fresh in his mind. So when he mentioned vegetarians (14:2), he was not talking about people who did not believe in killing animals and eating them. He was talking about people who were so concerned about potentially eating meat that had been sacrificed to a god that they preferred not to eat meat at all.

Several items of background are helpful here.[4] We should remember that meat was somewhat of a luxury. Most ancient people only ate meat during city festivals, so not eating meat was nothing like the sacrifice it would be for many today. And most of the meat available in a city probably came from nearby temples. Ancient sacrifices did not consume the whole animal. Even after priests and the family of the one making the sacrifice had eaten their fill, a good deal of meat was left over. Since it could not be refrigerated for later, it might easily make its way to the market place, where people would buy it.[5]

So should a believer in the one God of Israel eat meat that had been sacrificed to another god? Was it important to find out where the meat you were about to buy or eat had come from? In Corinth, Paul took a "don't ask" approach—do not ask where the meat in the marketplace came from (1 Cor. 10:25). But do not eat if a person with a troubled conscience tells you the meat came from a temple—not because of your conscience but because of his or hers (1 Cor. 10:28–30).

NO STUMBLING BLOCKS

The important thing, as can be seen so clearly in Romans 14–15, is that you are thinking of other people and not putting a reason to stumble in front of them (Rom. 14:13). It is so easy for people whose conscience does not bother them on some issue to think of themselves as superior to those who are troubled by the same things. So on the Sabbath, Paul said some Gentiles were not worried about whether or not they set one day apart; they considered every day alike (14:5). They must not look down at their conservative Jewish or Gentile brothers and sisters who were concerned to observe sundown on Friday to sundown on Saturday as a Sabbath on which they did not work.

LIFE REFLECTIONS

Paul's principles are clear, immediately applicable to our day, and yet pervasively ignored by Christians today. Admittedly, it is not always easy for us to see which matters are truly disputable and which are nonnegotiable. The conservatives of Paul's day might easily have said, "Look, the Sabbath goes back to creation in Genesis. Look, it is one of the Ten Commandments." And amazingly, Paul did not seem to give it a second thought. In fact, Colossians almost denigrated those who worried about "a New Moon celebration or a Sabbath day" (Col. 2:16). So also today, there are no doubt issues where Christians come down hard on other Christians because of the letter of Scripture without realizing they have not caught its Spirit. The issue of women in ministry comes to mind.

But Paul's admonition in Romans 14 was far more directed at the liberal (with relation to the Jewish Law) than the conservative (in relation to the same law), even though Paul placed himself among the liberals in this argument. The person of strong conscience must not despise the person of weak conscience, even though he or she may be in the right. It is far more important for the church to be unified and edified than for it to be right on these sorts of matters. "Who are you to judge someone else's servant?" Paul said (Rom. 14:4). We stand or fall before our own master.

Finding the balance between things on which we should or should not judge our brothers and sisters is a matter of great care. The current spirit of the age is not to judge at all. But Paul did not model this extreme either, nor did Jesus. Jesus clearly had an indictment to bring to the leaders of Israel, and Paul did not shrink from pronouncing judgment on the man sleeping with his step-mother (1 Cor. 5:1–3). The Bible has no criticism for someone who would make a serial killer aware that he or she is displeasing God.

In Romans 2:1, Paul indicted the person who passes judgment on another when he or she is guilty of the same or similar sins. And later Paul indicted the person who condemns another believer on a matter of conviction when that other Christian's conscience is clear (14:3–4).

The problem, again, is that Christians regularly disagree on what is or is not a matter of personal conviction. For example, we find individuals who believe in Christ and consider themselves Christians, yet who would say their conscience is clear with regard to homosexual practice. Is this a disputable matter or one where Paul would expel a person from Christian fellowship?

It seems clear that Paul would have expelled such an individual from the church, given what he said in 1 Corinthians 5:11 and 6:9. But lest we think the clarity of Scripture makes such decisions obvious, we should remember that the Old Testament speaks much more emphatically and frequently about the importance of Sabbath observance than it does against homosexual sex (see Num. 15:32–36; Ezek. 20). I believe Paul was inspired to be able to distinguish between which issue was disputable and which was not. But we can rest assured that in Paul's day, the difference would not at all have been clear to a devout Jew.

DISTINGUISHING BETWEEN SINFUL
AND DISPUTABLE MATTERS

Christians disagree on many things, especially in a world where Protestantism has fragmented the church into tens of thousands of small groups. I grew up around Christians who thought that wearing jewelry or a woman wearing slacks were not disputable issues but practices every believer should avoid. We are always free to share our concerns with others if, as Paul says, our love is sincere (Rom. 12:9). However, one suspects that some concern sharing over the years has been little more than gossip with a critical spirit. With such a history, it is understandable that the current generation would refrain from almost any comment that could be perceived as judgmental.

It requires a significant level of discernment to distinguish between matters that are disputable and those that are not in the Christian faith. Perhaps we should consider as a disputable matter anything that does not clearly harm another person and over which people clearly devoted to Christ disagree. On these issues, we should agree to disagree and be charitable in spirit, "For we will all stand before God's judgment seat" (14:10) and "each of us will give an account of himself to God" (14:12). We should remember that we can be wrongly convinced. "Blessed are those who have no reason to condemn themselves because of what they approve" (14:22 NRSV). On these sorts of matters, Paul bid us leave it up to God.

"Let all be fully convinced in their own minds" (14:5 NRSV)—this is the key with regard to our position on disputable issues: that we are truly acting from faith. "Everything that does not come from faith is sin" (14:23). We can deceive and convince ourselves that we are free to do things about which we have significant doubt. This is the kind of doubter Paul had in mind in 14:23: the person who is not really convinced he or she can do what he or she says. I do not believe Paul was thinking of the person with a hyperactive conscience who feels guilty about most things. He meant the person who knows inside that what he or she proposes to do is wrong but pretends to be clear of conscience and does it anyway. While we should probably let the person get away with it, be assured that God knows what is in their hearts.

Paul left us here with a wonderful way to define sin. He described sin as the violation of some absolute standard. Sin is when we intentionally do something we know God does not want us to do. Sin and right living in this chapter are a matter of how we act in conjunction with what we are thinking, what we are intending. "I am fully convinced that no food is unclean in itself," Paul said (Rom. 14:14). Everything belongs to God anyway (1 Cor. 10:26), even that meat that someone thinks has been offered to a god. The problem is not in the food or even the act. It is what we are thinking when we do the act.

To be sure, we can unintentionally wrong others and sin against them. And we can have a sinful attitude without being fully aware of it, such as those who enjoy gossiping about others without realizing what their delight says about their heart. But the kind of sin with which God is most concerned is when we consciously and intentionally think or act in a way that we know does not please God, when we do not act in accordance with our faith.[6]

A teen once asked me how far he could go with a girl before he would go to hell. In one respect, he had already gone too far. His entire line of thought did not come from the perspective of faith in God. His question was not, "How can I live in a way that glorifies God?" but "How much can I get away with before God will send me to hell?" Faith asks what is most pleasing to God; sin asks how displeasing to God we can be and get away with it. A life without sin is a life in which our intentions are full of faith and our actions are full of love.

FOR FURTHER REFLECTION

1. If a transformed mind for Paul is to love one another, do you have a transformed mind? Read Romans 12–13 again, and ask what areas of your attitude might be improved. Do you think your life would change more if your ideas changed, or do you think your ideas would change more if you could put in place habits of virtue?

2. Who are the strong and weak in your community of faith, using Paul's descriptions as the way to define them? Do the strong look down on the weak for not being enlightened? Do the weak condemn the strong for being liberal? What needs to be changed? Can you think of a loving way to move in that direction, starting with yourself?

3. Can you think of any "stumbling blocks" you might be putting in front of others? Are there any areas where your freedom causes difficulties for others in their faith or in their lives?

4. Think back to Romans 1–11. How would you say the material in those chapters has prepared the way for this more concrete and practical instruction?

IN THE WORLD

LIVE AT PEACE

The second half of Romans not only addresses how believers should relate to each other, but we also find comments on how to relate to those outside the church. What Paul said in Romans 12:18 is some of the best advice you could get on the subject: "If it is possible, as far as it depends on you, live at peace with everyone." The problem is that it is not always possible to live at peace with others. If someone wants to pick a fight, then you simply cannot live at peace with him or her. It should be possible for you as a believer to live at peace with anyone through the power of the Holy Spirit, but because others often do not feel the same, sometimes you have to walk away, endure, or perhaps even go to war.

This last comment is a matter of debate among Christians. In our human mind, it seems impossible to picture a world where war or self-defense is not a necessary evil in some cases. Can I not shoot an intruder intent on killing or raping my spouse or children? Can a nation under attack not fight back? Can a nation not come to the aid of another country in dire need? Common sense tells us that fighting in these cases is a lamentable but virtuous thing to do.

At the same time, the biblical case is not nearly as strong as some imagine. Jesus' teaching in particular leans toward the pacifist, one who doesn't fight back. And some of the things Paul said in Romans 12 sound a lot like some of Jesus' teaching in the Sermon on the Mount (Matt. 5–7). For example, Paul said, "Bless those who persecute you; bless and do not curse. Rejoice with those who rejoice; mourn with those who mourn" (Rom. 12:14–15). These verses coincide with several elements in the Beatitudes of Matthew 5: "Blessed are those who mourn . . . blessed are those who are persecuted because of righteousness . . . rejoice and be glad, because great is your reward in heaven" (5:4, 10, 12). Jesus went on to say, "If someone strikes you on the right cheek, turn to him the other also" (5:39).

Some scholars thus suggest that Paul was alluding to Jesus' teaching here, especially when he said not to curse those who persecute you. Paul said, "Do not repay anyone evil for evil" (Rom. 12:17), and you are not to seek revenge for the bad things people do to you (12:19). Rather, Paul said to let God take care of it. God is the one who gets to avenge wrongdoing. It is his to repay (12:20). We, by contrast, are to feed and give drink to our enemy when he or she needs it. We are to "overcome evil with good" (12:21).

Perhaps another key factor to take into account is that Paul was not speaking of governments at this point, just as Jesus was not addressing the question of human authorities. Both Jesus and Paul were addressing individuals and their relationships with one another. Indeed, Paul went on in Romans 13 to speak of the role of human authority as God's servant, "an agent of wrath to bring punishment on the wrongdoer" (13:4). In other words, Paul implied that human governments can be agents of God's judgment even in this world, that God can bring vengeance on the unjust through worldly powers.

Certainly Paul knew that worldly authorities often got it wrong. How many times had he been beaten and imprisoned by the time he wrote Romans? We thus should not take what Paul says in Romans 13 as an absolute statement, "For rulers hold no terror for those who do right, but for those who do wrong. Do you want to be free from fear of the one in authority? Then do what is right and he [or she] will commend you" (13:3). I suspect the knee-jerk reaction for someone who knows even a little history is something like, "Yeah, right!" Was someone reading Paul's mail, and he knew it? Was not the emperor at the time Nero, who would eventually have Paul put to death?[1]

Nevertheless, human authority is supposed to work in this way. Paul shockingly said that "there is no authority except that which God has established. The authorities that exist have been established by God" (13:1). Kings like Louis XIV of France used this passage to argue for their divine right to have absolute authority over their people. Various Christians of the 1600s used these verses to argue that God commands those under human authority not to rebel against them. As Paul said, the one "who rebels against the authority is rebelling against what God has instituted, and those who do so will bring judgment on themselves" (13:2).

Paul gave no contingency in these verses, as if we only have to submit to worldly authorities when they are doing what they are supposed to do for us. Indeed, the earliest Christians seemed to assume that they would suffer unjustly under human authorities. The entire letter of 1 Peter was a defensive strategy for believers oppressed in the current age, including slaves and wives in less than ideal situations.[2] We can wonder whether Paul would have ever supported America's Revolutionary

War; John Wesley himself believed it was not God's will. Paul accepted institutions like slavery and the headship of the husband as the temporary state of things, even if such structures would not exist in the kingdom of God.

However, we also need to consider two significant factors of Paul's context that impacted his acceptance of these skewed social structures. The first is the fact that Paul expected Jesus to return from heaven very soon. By the time he wrote Romans, he may have realized he would not live to see Christ's return, but most likely, he thought it would happen soon: "The hour has come for you to wake up from your slumber, because our salvation is nearer now than when we first believed. The night is nearly over; the day is almost here" (13:11–12). Paul thought the first order of business was getting the good news out to the whole world. Changing the social structures of the world was not on his radar.

A second consideration is that the earliest Christians were in no position of empowerment to where they could change the social structures of their age. Indeed, Christ would do exactly this deed himself when he returned. There would be no slave in the kingdom and there would be no subordination of wives to husbands in marriage (see 1 Cor. 7:21–24, 29–31). These simply were not the priority or focus of the earliest believers. It is doubtful that Paul would have ever supported bloodshed to fight for these sorts of things. So our application of Paul's words in Romans must take these aspects of Paul's context into account when translating them into our contexts today.

SUBMIT TO AUTHORITY

Certainly few if any Christians would understand Paul's teaching here to be absolute, that is, without exception. We do not believe we must obey human authority in every case. Indeed, it is quite clear that the earliest Christians themselves often came to a point where they had to choose between serving God and obeying human authorities. Acts 4:19 presents Peter respectfully asking the Jewish ruling council to "judge for [themselves] whether it [was] right in God's sight to obey [them] rather than God."[3] There is a time and place for civil disobedience when God's will is at stake.

However, the current climate in the West is probably too quick to disobey. For example, a number of Christian ministers do not pay taxes, supposedly as a matter of Christian conscience. The United States government allows for this possibility if the minister elects it from the beginning of his or her ministry. What is peculiar is that both Jesus (Mark 12:17; Matt. 17:24–27) and Paul (Rom. 13:7) tell their audiences to pay taxes. When you consider how corrupt and unjust the use of Roman taxes were in that day, no one in the Western world today has a biblical basis to argue that they should not pay taxes because they disagree with where the money is going.

The freedoms we enjoy in the Western world are great, and we must constantly thank God for them. But let us not mistake the self-oriented, individualistic focus of our culture for the biblical mindset. Jesus and Paul said we are bound as Christians to look more to the needs of others than to our own individual rights (Matt. 25:41–46; Phil. 2:3). Acts portrays the early church as far more prone to share their possessions as to keep them (Acts 2:45; see also 1 John 3:17). Our orientation must not be to keep all we can for ourselves, but to help as many others as possible.

Certainly we can debate how to help others best. James Dobson once popularized the idea that love must be tough.[4] His basic claim was that love does not always give a person what he or she wants. It may actually be better for others to let them experience the consequences of their actions in the hope that they will become better. In that sense, simply giving to others will not always be the best way to help them. By now the old proverb about fishing is well-known: Give someone a fish, and you have fed him or her once; teach someone how to fish, and you have fed him or her for a lifetime.

In our world, we have created a new issue. Western societies have gone at least half way in providing food and resources for the needy. But we have sometimes left such individuals with no desire to fish. The needy of Jesus' day were so desperate that they would have likely fished at any opportunity. No doubt the poor of today in developing nations would love nothing less than to work to feed themselves and their families. Immigrants to America today are some of the hardest working individuals you can find. Unfortunately, at times, Western democracies have only partially empowered the disempowered and left some of them in a halfway state that is neither sufficient nor motivating to do something about it. The loving thing in such cases may be neither simply to provide fish nor opportunities to learn to fish. In some instances, they may need to want to fish.

But none of this is an excuse to abandon the needy. God loved us when we were his enemies, when we were still sinners (Rom. 5:8). So those who use the current state of things as an excuse to do nothing are clearly in the wrong. What we should do to help others may change depending on the circumstances, but the drive to help others, even to the point of personal sacrifice, is a Christian absolute, without exception.

LIFE REFLECTIONS

Here we must look at some of the excuses Christians have developed when presented with the core Christian value of loving others in material ways. One is that Christians should help others, but only those within the church. But the Bible will not support such exclusivity. Even in ancient Israel, consideration was made for the hungry foreigner in the land (see Deut. 14:29).

The parable of the good Samaritan (Luke 10:25–37) itself intended to obliterate any pretense to exclusivity a person might use to defend not helping his or her neighbor. Its point was that a person could not redefine who one's neighbor was in order to get out of helping others. This is the very thing a person who uses this excuse is doing, trying to say that a non-believer is not his or her neighbor. What a telltale sign of how out of sync the Christian who has no interest in helping the poor is from the very heart of Jesus' message!

Galatians 6:10 may put a priority on doing good to other believers: "Therefore, as we have opportunity, let us do good to all people, especially to those who belong to the family of believers." But Paul situated helping other Christians in the context of what we must do in general for everyone. He put no artificial limits on those for whom we can do good. The very heart of a Christian is the impulse to benefit others, even to the point of personal sacrifice. This is exactly the message of Paul's teaching on the strong and weak in Romans 14. It is not about what we have coming to us or what our rights are. It is about building up and thinking of others.

This excuse naturally leads to another: only Christians should be in the business of doing good for others, not the government. Again, it is hard to imagine that the Bible stands in any way as the origin for this idea. We can certainly debate how well governments help others. We can use our incredible rights as citizens to steer how governments help others. But we have no biblical basis to say that governments shouldn't try to help others. Paul flatly said that human authority is "God's servant to do you good" (Rom. 13:4).

Certainly, human and divine authority were closely related in the Old Testament, since Israel was ideally governed by God's revealed law. Psalm 72 pictured the king of Israel delivering the needy who cry out (72:12), the poor of his people (72:4).[5] Certainly the New Testament saw the Christian community as self-contained and far removed from the worldly powers. The Roman Empire was irrelevant at best (Mark 12:16–17; 1 Cor. 6:1), and evil at worst (Rev. 18).

What the New Testament did not do was try to stop worldly powers from doing good. Indeed, the Bible more than once suggested that God can do good through worldly powers. The most obvious example is in Isaiah 45:1–4, where God used the Persian king Cyrus to return Israel to Jerusalem. It is this posture that Paul also took in Romans 13. Human authority rightly punishes crime, for example, and is "an agent of wrath to bring punishment on the wrongdoer" (Rom. 13:3–4). Interestingly, by mentioning that human authorities "bear the sword" (13:4) in God's service, Paul assumed the legitimacy of capital punishment.[6]

We cannot make recourse to the Bible or Christianity to argue against government programs to help others, whether at home or abroad. That debate we must hold completely on the merits of each individual instance. It is not somehow more Christian to argue that only the church should help the needy. Indeed, the church does not and cannot help others to the degree that governments can, and Christian organizations could not do as much good as they actually do without the government's help.

A final argument that is sometimes used is an artifact of American history and, perhaps to a large degree, an explanation for why so many Christians can go against the clear tenor of Scripture on this sort of topic. In the early 1900s, helping poor Christians became associated with what was called a "social gospel." Those who most emphasized helping others were considered liberal Christians, because they were often Christians who questioned things like the virgin birth or the divinity of Christ. As is often the case, we disassociate ourselves not only with the things we disagree with in others, but also with good aspects of their thinking that we might agree with. Such was the case in mainstream evangelical circles of the mid-twentieth century with regard to helping the poor and needy.

The Wesleyan tradition did not fully participate in this reaction, nor did Christians from other countries. And it would be hard to say that this overreaction had much impact on the Salvation Army or the Free Methodist Church. (The Wesleyan-Methodist tradition was born with an emphasis on social action, abolition, and the women's rights movements.) Thankfully, our isolation from the broader discussion largely kept our food pantries intact. If we have been affected, it has only been of late because of the political climate of the last few decades.

But it is essential to realize the social gospel message of mainline churches in the early twentieth century was not a reaction against the truth. It was all that was left of the truth. After so many mainline churches had lost their belief in miracles, in the divinity of Christ, and the revelation of Scripture, all they had left was the Christian ethos of loving our neighbor. There was nothing wrong with these drives. It was all they had left of Christianity, the only thing that motivated them to continue to call themselves Christians. Let us not be deceived by the accidents of history into abandoning one of the central messages of the Bible.

We are therefore to submit to human authority. This is a key New Testament message, whether it be to parents, teachers, bosses, church leaders, or government, we are to be respectful and peaceful. Certainly there is a time for disobedience. Certainly democratic systems give immense room to disagree and work for change. Today, we can move our nations closer to the kingdom than the earliest apostles were able to do. We do not have to be in an adversarial stance with human authority. We should strive not to be in conflict with human authority as much as is possible.

The principle is thus neither withdrawal nor assimilation. We are to be the church. The context in which we find ourselves may sometimes lead to separation, sometimes to involvement. It may lead us to submission or civil disobedience. Governments can do good and evil. And no matter what the government does, we are to be the church.

FOR FURTHER REFLECTION

1. Do you think that human authority, like governments, is (a) mostly corrupt and does evil; (b) mostly good as servants of God; (c) morally neutral, neither good nor bad; or (d) good or bad depending on the time, place, and people involved? Why or why not?

2. When do you think it is appropriate to disobey human authority? How long do you think you should remain silent when you see human authority acting unjustly? How certain do you think you need to be before disobeying or speaking out?

3. Do you agree with the claim that there are some acts of goodness toward the needy that we—either as individuals or as churches—will never be as well equipped to address as governments? For example, do you think individuals and churches could ever bring disaster relief on the scale of major earthquakes and tsunamis as well as governments? Could individuals or churches ever evacuate people effectively like governments? Could relief agencies accomplish the good they do without the subsidies they receive from governments?

10

AN EARLY
FAITH COMMUNITY

A LETTER OF RECOMMENDATION

The list of names at the end of Romans may not seem inspiring at first, but it has many tantalizing nuggets, especially when you think that we are looking at a community of faith just like us. Think about the people you worship with each Sunday. Close your eyes and imagine you are in a worship service right now. Look around with your mind's eye. You know where everyone sits. You know the older couple that sits over to the right and the young couple that sits down front.

It is this sort of list that we are reading in Romans 16, except they met in houses rather than church buildings, and we are looking at believers scattered across a city rather than a single local assembly of believers. Romans 16 gives us a truly amazing peek into some of the social dynamics of the earliest churches, especially those associated with Paul's mission.[1] People have often wondered how Paul could know so many people at Rome when he had never visited there. Indeed, the last time we ran into Priscilla and Aquila (Rom. 16:3), they were in Ephesus (see 1 Cor. 16:19; cf. 2 Tim. 4:19). Many Paul experts wonder if Romans 16 was originally sent to Ephesus rather than Rome.

This may seem like a strange suggestion, that the last chapter of Romans is actually a letter of recommendation originally sent somewhere else. One reason ideas like this seem so strange is because we can read the Bible so much as God's word to us that we forget its books were originally written to people who have been dead for two centuries. We can easily have a "what you see is what you get" expectation that can make us resistant to thorough study. We have to remind ourselves that scholars who seek the original meaning are simply asking a different question: How did these books look to their first audiences? Certainly we should not look for such theories just to come up with something new. But neither should we resist them when they actually make better sense of the evidence we have.

We tend to picture the prophet Isaiah sitting down to write the book with his name from beginning to end in one sitting, with God dictating each word as he went along. But it is not likely that the book came together in this way.[2] Even with a letter like Romans, we should think of a process of at least several days of writing, quite possibly weeks, with a rough draft first.[3] Writers generally kept a copy of their letters, as well as sending one. With this in mind, we can imagine Paul writing to the Romans (Rom. 1–15) and the Ephesians (Eph. 16) at the same time in Corinth. The letter he sent to Rome had the first fifteen chapters of our current book of Romans. Then Romans 16 was a second letter, a letter of recommendation for Phoebe to the church at Ephesus. Romans as it currently stands might be the copy Paul kept with him.

No important item of faith is at stake here. All things being equal, I believe the evidence leans toward Romans 16 being a separate letter. It is certainly possible that Paul knew such a large number of people in Rome, as well as the specific house churches they attended. It is also possible that Epenetus, the first convert to Christianity in Asia Minor, where Ephesus was, had moved to Rome for some reason (Rom. 16:5). It is possible that Priscilla and Aquila (16:3), who were in Ephesus just a few years earlier (1 Cor. 16:19), had moved to Rome only to be located back in Ephesus again in 2 Timothy 4:19. It is possible that Rufus' mother had been a mother to Paul at some point in the past, before moving to Rome (Rom. 16:13). It is possible, but these details clearly fit Ephesus better, and the only thing to keep us from drawing that conclusion is the current packaging of Romans. Even here, the manuscript evidence suggests that some ancient copies of Romans circulated without chapter 16.

Romans 16 is a letter of recommendation for a woman named Phoebe, who was a deacon (*diakonos*) at the port village of Cenchrea, about five miles southeast of Corinth. It was a common practice to take a letter of recommendation such as this one when going to a location where they did not know you. In this case, the church at Ephesus (or Rome) would know that they could trust Phoebe because of Paul's letter. They would know that she was who she said she was and that they could incorporate her into the ministry of the city.

Those who do not believe women ministered in Paul's churches are keen to reinterpret the word *diakonos* in 16:1. They want to translate it merely as *servant* or perhaps even as *deaconess*. But this is the very same word Paul used in Philippians 1:1 of ministry leaders at Philippi. It is the masculine word used of Timothy as a servant of Christ (1 Tim. 4:6). In that passage and elsewhere, it is used to refer to the official role of a deacon.

Therefore, we can be certain above all that the word does not mean deaconess. It is the same form of the word used in 1 Timothy 3:8–13 where the qualifications for such a position were given. Further, since Phoebe was the *diakonos* of a specific house church in Romans 16:1, the burden of proof is on the person who wants to argue she did not hold a formal leadership role in the church there.

What was this role? Churches often reference Acts 6:1–7 as a picture of what a deacon did in an ancient church. In Acts 6, Peter and the Jerusalem church appointed individuals to take care of the distribution of food to widows so that they could continue to provide spiritual leadership to the community.[4] It may be that this passage gives us an accurate picture of what deacons did in the early church, but it is also important to recognize that the word *deacon* never appears in Acts 6. So we cannot be entirely sure that Acts 6 shows us what deacons did.

Nevertheless, it seems clear enough that deacons played a subordinate role to overseers in local house churches and Christian communities. They are listed second both in Philippians 1:1 and in the qualification descriptions of 1 Timothy 3. The fact that the word can mean "servant" suggests that deacons may very well have performed roles like those we hear about in Acts 6.

The rest of Romans 16 makes it abundantly clear that women did play a significant role in Paul's churches. If we do not have this impression, it is because it is popular to read Paul's writings through the lens of 1 Timothy. But 1 Timothy is the exception on the subject of women in ministry, not the rule. Paul's earlier writings, as well as Acts, picture an early church where the ministry roles of men and women were not clearly distinguished from each other.

Almost a third of those greeted in Romans 16 were women, perhaps implying that about a third of the leadership in the church at Ephesus (or Rome) were women. Not all of these women were in husband-wife teams (such as, Mary, Tryphena, Tryphosa, and Persis), as if Paul only mentioned women attached to a man. Indeed, he did not mention the wives of most of the men, as if he was only greeting these women on a social level. His criterion was that these women had "worked very hard" (Rom. 16:6, 12).

Indeed, in the most significant husband-wife ministry team, Paul mentioned the woman first, Priscilla. Earlier, her husband's name only appeared before Priscilla's in relation to their move from Rome to Corinth (Acts 18:2). In the passage where they are actually engaged in ministry when she and her husband instructed Apollos in the way of Christ more accurately (18:24–28), Priscilla's name appeared first. Similarly, the only instance where Paul put Aquila's name first was in his greeting in 1 Corinthians 16:19, addressed to a church apparently having problems with some of its wives.[5]

Perhaps most startling in this chapter is Paul's greeting to a husband and wife by the names of Andronicus and Junia. Our interest in them would be piqued if for no other reason than that they are said to be "prominent among the apostles" (Rom. 16:7 CEB). What does this statement mean? Does it mean the apostles were well-acquainted with them or that they were notable apostles themselves?

First, what was an apostle? In Paul's understanding, an apostle was someone to whom the risen Lord appeared and whom he sent out to proclaim the good news that Jesus is the Christ (see 1 Cor. 9:1). Paul thought of himself as the last of such apostles, the last to whom the risen Lord appeared, some three years after Jesus' resurrection (15:8).[6] Paul thus did not in any way restrict apostleship to the eleven original disciples. For example, he referred to Barnabas as an apostle (9:6).

Could Andronicus and Junia qualify? Paul told us that "they were in Christ before [he] was" (Rom. 16:7), so they fit the time frame of an apostle. The fact that they were at the very least known by the original apostles implies that they were from Palestine. They were Paul's "kins-men" (NASB), by which Paul probably meant that they were Jews. They had been imprisoned with Paul, which implied that they were Christian leaders. Perhaps we might more appropriately ask what would keep us from understanding them to be apostles. Would not all interpreters agree that these two were apostles if it were not for the female name?

Some manuscripts of Romans have Junias, a man's name, instead of Junia here. The best explanation is that some copyists were increasingly uncomfortable with the idea of a female apostle and so added *s* to make her male. One of the most basic rules of figuring out the original wording of a text is to ask how the wording might have changed over time. We know that Christianity, if anything, became less supportive of women in leadership over time rather than more supportive. So it is easy to imagine that someone changed the name from feminine to masculine. It is difficult to imagine it going the other way around.

We will return to the question of women in the third and final volume of this series, *Paul—Prisoner of Hope*, when we look at the letter known as 1 Timothy. As you might guess from our discussion of Romans 16, I see 1 Timothy as the exception in its tone and sense of women, in contrast to Paul's earlier writings. Even 1 Corinthians, with its correctives to some problems relating to wives, would not lead us in the direction in which 1 Timothy is currently leading so many in the church today. Instead, what we see in Acts and here in Romans 16 is that women worked alongside men in the spreading of the gospel and the leading of local house churches and communities of faith.

There is no evidence in Romans 16 that women only led other women. Just as in 1 Corinthians 11, women prophesied in the presence of men in public worship. The picture we get from Romans 16 is that leadership developed naturally in these churches. In some instances, women led or hosted the house churches. In some instances, men led the churches. In other instances, husband-wife teams led the house churches, with whoever having gifts of leadership probably taking the lead.

If I were to guess how God would do it, this is what I would predict. Some men are natural-born leaders and full of spiritual insight. And so are some women. If I tried to predict what God would do, I would guess he would have the gifted leaders lead and those with insight teach and share.

By contrast, the idea that God would have the men always be the leaders or give the insight simply because of their physical anatomy, would be quite peculiar indeed! I will contend in the next volume that this is a fascinating example of God's people lacking good common spiritual sense. Like some of the Pharisees pictured in Matthew, it is an example of God's well-intentioned people (and some perhaps not so well-intentioned) getting wrapped up in the letter and the details and losing sight of God's underlying principles and goals.

THE ENDING OF ROMANS

If Romans 16 was sent to Ephesus, then the part sent to Rome might have originally ended at 15:33: "The God of peace be with you all. Amen." Interestingly, the earliest copy of Paul's letters, which dates to around A.D. 200, has the doxology of Romans 16:25–27 exactly here, at the end of Romans 15. This location may indicate that some very early copies of Romans ended there.[7] Early manuscripts of Romans are all over the map in how they end. Many early ones have this doxology right after Romans 16, as it is in our Bibles. Others have it both here and at the end of chapter 14. Some do not have it after chapter 16 but have it at the end of chapter 14. Then some do not have it at all.

The originality of the doxology itself faces serious questions. It does not sound like the rest of Romans in many respects (for example, "the revelation of the mystery hidden for long ages past, but now revealed and made known through the prophetic writings by the command of the eternal God" (16:25–26). It does not appear in all manuscripts and widely differs in where it is placed in those that have it. To top it off, some manuscripts of Romans have 16:20 after verse 23: "The grace of our Lord Jesus be with you." It is as if they were hinting that earlier copies of Romans ended here and did not have the doxology. Most scholars do not believe this doxology was originally a part of Romans.

Here is what I wonder: The letter Paul sent to Rome ended with Romans 15:33. Romans 16 was sent to Ephesus as a letter of recommendation for Phoebe and a greeting of the churches there. Meanwhile, an early Christian named Origen (ca. A.D. 200) implied that a man named Marcion (ca. A.D. 150) had deleted the last two chapters. Therefore, by the end of the A.D. 100s, there may have been three versions of Romans: one that ended after chapter 14, one that ended after chapter 15, and one that ended after chapter 16. All three of these seemed to lack a proper ending.

Once again, these variations should not trouble us. This discussion is only about historical details, not about the true, theological message. Indeed, God apparently has not had any problem with the doxology of Romans these last eighteen hundred years. These observations can lead to some very helpful reflection. Why is knowing the reason a book like Romans or Mark ended so important to some of us? To be sure, it is a legitimate question, and why would we not want to know as much as we can about every word God spoke in every time and every place?

But when we look at texts like the ending of Mark (16:9–20) or this doxology in Romans (16:25–27), can we find any fault with them? Do they not fit with the things God has said in the rest of Scripture? Most importantly, have not Christians read and heard God's voice in them for almost two thousand years? Maybe the question of the original wording is less important than the fact that these passages have been read as Scripture for almost the entire history of the church, indeed since even before Christians agreed on exactly which books even belonged in Scripture![8] If it was good enough for God to leave in for two thousand years, perhaps it is good enough for us to continue to include in our Bibles.[9]

FOR FURTHER REFLECTION

1. What do you make of the women involved in leadership in Paul's churches? Does this fact surprise you? Do you agree with this interpretation?

2. What do you make of the suggestion that Romans 16 was meant for Ephesus or that the ending of Romans is not original? Do these things bother you? Enough to reject them? What do you think the proper perspective is on the difference between how the Bible looks to us and how it looked to the original audiences? What do you think the proper mix of understanding is between the human and inspired dimensions of Scripture?

3. Some Christians picture inspiration something like dictation: the author sat down and God gave the precise words to write from start to finish. As you have read through this book and (hopefully) the previous one, you have seen the human element as well. For example, Romans 16:22 mentions Tertius, the secretary who recorded Romans. While these facts do not contradict the inspiration of Scripture, they might require a different understanding of how inspiration took place—one that can take into account the human personalities, processes, and situations in which these letters originated. How has your understanding of inspiration changed or remained the same as you have worked through this book?

NOTES

PREFACE

1. Krister Stendahl, "Paul and the Introspective Conscience of the West," in *Paul among Jews and Gentiles* (Minneapolis, Minn.: Augsberg Fortress, 1976), 78–96.

2. E. P. Sanders, *Paul and Palestinian Judaism: A Comparison of Patterns of Religion* (Minneapolis, Minn.: Fortress Press, 1977).

3. You can now find a collection of Dunn's most important articles on this subject in James. D. G. Dunn, *The New Perspective on Paul* (Grand Rapids, Mich.: Eerdmans, 2005).

4. Probably the best place to get his point of view is in N. T. Wright, *Justification: God's Plan and Paul's Vision* (Downers Grove, Ill.: InterVarsity Press Academic, 2009).

5. Robert Jewett, *Romans: A Commentary* (Minneapolis, Minn.: Fortress Press, 2006).

CHAPTER 1

1. As we will see in chapter 5, it is not at all clear that Romans 16 was meant for Rome. Since it is currently packaged with the rest of Romans, we need a good reason to speculate that it was not meant for Rome. The

question, however, is not how the text came to us, but how it came to the original audiences.

Four reasons point toward a different destination for Romans 16 than for the rest of the letter: (1) variations in the ancient copies of Romans; (2) the fact that Priscilla and Aquila were at Ephesus, not Rome, in the surrounding letters; (3) the fact that Paul would have to know so many people at a place he had never been; and (4) one of those Paul mentioned was the first convert of Asia. For these reasons, it seems likely that Romans 16 was first sent to Ephesus rather than Rome, as I discuss in chapter 10.

2. Some such as myself suspect that Paul's persecutions especially targeted Greek-speaking Jewish believers like those mentioned in Acts 6.

3. We will look at 2 Thessalonians in the next volume of this series, *Paul—Prisoner of Hope*.

4. Kenneth Schenck, *Paul—Messenger of Grace* (Indianapolis, Ind.: Wesleyan Publishing House, 2010).

5. The book of Acts, in its tendency to emphasize order, seems to emphasize Peter as the initiator of the Gentile mission in Acts 10 and at the Jerusalem Council of Acts 15. Paul probably did not tell the story the same way. Indeed, he saw Peter at Antioch more as an obstacle to the Gentile mission (Gal. 2:11).

6. The verse is in the famous suffering servant passage in Isaiah, which many early Christians seem to have read in relation to Christ's sufferings on the cross.

7. It is intriguing that Acts never mentions this offering, even though it was an incredibly big deal for Paul (see Rom. 15:25–27; 1 Cor. 16:1–4; 2 Cor. 8–9). Acts gives us a lot of information that fits the framework of a delegation with an offering but, strangely, does not mention the offering itself. We have to wonder whether the Jerusalem church did not accept the offering or if the money ended up being used in some other way. Some suggest that Paul used the offering to pay for the purification rites of the men with a vow in Acts 21:24.

8. If one dates Galatians early, then the incident at Antioch would have taken place before the Jerusalem Council of Acts 15.

9. Dale Carnegie, *How to Win Friends and Influence People* (New York: Simon & Schuster, 1936), 123.

10. Philip Melanchthon, *Loci Communes*, trans. by C. L. Hill (Boston: Meador, 1944), 69.

CHAPTER 2

1. The first volume of this series, *Paul—Messenger of Grace*, has a running series in the notes of books that one might read to become an expert on Paul. One of the key books on that list is E. P. Sanders, *Paul and Palestinian Judaism: A Comparison of Patterns of Religion* (London: SCM, 1977).

2. Sanders, *Paul and Palestinian Judaism*, 552. I would not want to use Sanders' terms here. Christianity at this time is still a form of Judaism.

3. Ibid., 443–444.

4. A famous line in an early second-century Jewish book in Greek called the *Letter of Aristeas* says that, "To prevent our being perverted by contact with others or by mixing with bad influences, he [God] hedged us in on all sides with strict observances connected with meat and drink and touch and hearing and sight, after the manner of the law." R. J. H. Shutt, "Letter of Aristeas," in *The Old Testament Pseudepigrapha, Vol. 2: Expansions of the Old Testament and Legends, Wisdom and Philosophical Literature, Prayers, Psalms and Odes, Fragments of Lost Judeo-Hellenistic Works*, ed. James H. Charlesworth (New York: Doubleday, 1985), 22.

5. This is one of the key insights of the "new perspective" on Paul and Judaism that has developed over the last thirty years. Judaism never believed that a person could earn a right standing with God. And as Sanders pointed out, keeping the Jewish Law was not about getting in to Israel or the people of God; it was about staying in the people of God; Sanders, *Paul and Palestinian Judaism*, 420.

It is fascinating that Lutheran and Calvinist interpreters are those who have perhaps most equated Judaism's emphasis on works as a sign of "works-righteousness," an attempt to earn salvation. And it is equally fascinating that it was someone who grew up Methodist (Sanders) who most promoted the idea that Jewish Law-keeping was much more in response to God's grace toward and covenant with Israel than it was an attempt to earn a righteous status.

6. N. T. Wright does an excellent job of focusing the good news of the gospel on the fact that Jesus is King (see *What Saint Paul Really Said: Was Paul of Tarsus the Real Founder of Christianity?* [Grand Rapids, Mich.: Eerdmans, 1997], 39–62). He is also quite insistent that the word *gospel* does not include salvation. It is not clear to me why he would be so dogmatic on this point, when surely the implications of Christ's kingship might easily be part of what Paul included within the "good news."

7. If we are to get into Paul's head on these sorts of things, we have to forget for a minute some of what we know as Christians from God's continued revelation these last two thousand years. On the one hand, it would

be foolish for us to reinvent the wheel. God helped the Christians of the first five centuries to unpack and unfold the significance of Jesus, asking questions that went way beyond anything on the minds of the first Christians. How exactly does Jesus' humanity and divinity fit together, for example? The answers to which God led Christians are the common understandings of the Trinity and dual nature of Christ. It would be silly—not to mention dangerous—to try to rehash these questions all over again.

But the legitimacy, probably even primacy, of these Christian readings do not change the fact that what was going on in Paul's head when he wrote words like "declared the Son of God with power" (Rom. 1:4 NASB) had their first meaning in what words meant in Paul's day. For example, at the time of Paul, "Son of God" was an expression that could be used of any of the kings of the Old Testament and language of "bowing the knee" (worship) was appropriate to them. The royal verses Paul and other New Testament authors apply to Jesus were applied to Old Testament human kings as well.

So 2 Samuel 7:14 was originally about Solomon and implied that he was God's representative, a human representative of God's authority on the throne of Israel. When Hebrews 1:5 quoted this verse, its author may not have been thinking quite as much about Jesus' divinity as we do when we read it. We know Jesus is fully God, begotten of God the Father from eternity past. But it is not at all clear that God had led the New Testament authors to figure this much out at that time. Christians came to these understandings through the continued direction of the Holy Spirit as they reflected further on the words of Scripture.

8. Ephesians 2:8, which says, "You have been saved," is quite unusual for Paul's writings. As we will see in the next book in the series, *Paul—Prisoner of Hope*, Ephesians is not typical of Paul's writings in the varied imagery it uses. For this reason, John McRay's *Paul: His Life and Teaching* (Grand Rapids, Mich.: Baker Academic, 2003), while well-intentioned, is probably misleading in its portrait of Paul's theology, because it uses Ephesians as its basis for summarizing it.

9. In the East, most Christians were Orthodox beginning in the year 1054, when the Eastern and Western churches formally split from each other.

10. In fact, most translations translate *dikaiosynē* as *justice* in Romans 3:26.

11. *Simul iustus et peccator, semper repentans.* You can find the phrase in *Lectures on Galatians*, *Luther Works*, vol. 26, trans. by J. J. Pelikan (Moorhead, Minn.: Concordia College, 1962), 232.

12. Luther's understanding on justification had a major impact on John Wesley. Wesley's understanding of justification is basically that of Luther.

It is on the question of sanctification after justification that they differed dramatically.

13. Certainly in Paul's earlier writings like 1 Thessalonians and 1 Corinthians, this judgment would seem to take place at the time of Christ's return and the resurrection. Most would say this timing continued throughout all Paul's writings. Some have argued, however, that 2 Corinthians sees this judgment taking place right after death and that Paul's sense of the immediacy of reward shifted a little during his time at Ephesus.

14. Here I am going to add to the list of key books on Paul: Richard Hays, *Echoes of Scripture in the Letters of Paul* (New Haven, Conn.: Yale University Press, 1989). In this book, Hays explores passages in Paul that may echo passages from the Old Testament. For him, an echo is something weaker than a full-blown allusion, where an author quite clearly and intentionally points toward a specific Old Testament (or other) text.

15. The next verse reads, "He has remembered his love and his faithfulness to the house of Israel; all the ends of the earth have seen the salvation of our God" (Ps. 98:3).

16. Many will know that Hebrew poetry does not rhyme sounds, but ideas. The verses discussed here use synonymous parallelism, where one line is followed by another that roughly says the same thing.

17. For example, the Dead Sea Scrolls speak of God's righteousness in similar terms: "If I stumble, the mercies of God shall be my salvation always; and if I fall in the sin of the flesh, in the justice of God . . . shall my judgment be . . . he will judge me in the justice of his truth, and in his plentiful goodness always atone for my sins; in his justice he will cleanse me from the uncleanness of the human being" (1QS11.12); Florentino G. Martínez and Eibert J. C. Tigchelar, trans., *The Dead Sea Scrolls Study Edition*, vol. 1 (Grand Rapids, Mich.: Eerdmans, 1997), 99.

18. See Andrew Newberg and Mark Waldman, *How God Changes Your Brain: Breakthrough Findings from a Leading Neuroscientist* (New York: Ballantine, 2009), 131–146.

19. The idea that God the Father might learn something on any level by becoming human or dying on the cross implies that he was not truly omniscient beforehand. A God who creates everything out of nothing would know everything, including what it feels like to sin.

20. If God knows everything at every point of his existence, then he cannot literally change his mind. Such pictures of God were very intelligible to the ancients, and God used them to speak to ancient Israel. However, from the standpoint of fully developed Christian understanding, such pictures are still too much like Zeus or Marduk.

21. Another book to add to the list of books to master Paul: Joel D. Green and Mark D. Baker, *Recovering the Scandal of the Cross: Atonement in the New Testament & Contemporary Contexts* (Downers Grove, Ill.: IVP Academic, 2000). The example of the prodigal son is often used in response to a rigid view of penal substitution.

CHAPTER 3

1. For example, one Qumran hymn says, "What is flesh compared to this? . . . He is in iniquity from his maternal womb, and in guilt of unfaithfulness right to old age" (1QH12.29–30); Florentino G. Martínez and Eibert J. C. Tigchelar, trans., *The Dead Sea Scrolls Study Edition*, vol. 1 (Grand Rapids, Mich.: Eerdmans, 1997), 170–171.

2. The prescript or greetings of Romans are in 1:1–7. Then the thanksgiving section continues at least through verse 15, where Paul thanks God for the Romans. Romans 1:16–17 are then the key verses of the letter.

3. We know that Psalm 8 was featured in Paul's thinking about Adam, because he alluded to it in 1 Corinthians 15 when he said that God was putting everything under Christ's feet (1 Cor. 15:27). Hebrews 2:5–11, which was probably written by someone associated with the Pauline mission, may give us a fuller version of Paul's thinking here.

4. This was one of the main points in Krister Stendahl, "Paul and the Introspective Conscience of the West," in *Paul Among Jews and Gentiles* (Minneapolis, Minn.: Fortress, 1976), 78–96. I consider this chapter one of the most significant pieces ever written on Paul.

5. This is a debated interpretation of Romans 2:14–15. A good argument for this interpretation can be found in Robert W. Wall, J. Paul Sampley, and N. T. Wright, *The New Interpreter's Bible: Acts—First Corinthians*, vol. 10 (Nashville: Abingdon, 2002), 441–442.

6. Perhaps the best-known proponent of this interpretation is Richard B. Hays, *The Faith of Jesus Christ: The Narrative Substructure of Galatians 3:1–4:11*, 2nd ed. (Grand Rapids, Mich.: Eerdmans, 2002). This book is another tool in mastering Paul.

7. The experts are divided on the issue, and the Greek is genuinely ambiguous. The best-known proponent of the traditional reading "faith in Jesus" is James D. G. Dunn, whose rebuttal is printed at the end of Hays, *Faith*, 249–271.

8. Some of the specific details that led me to this conclusion are the following. First, notice how redundant Paul's thought is in Galatians if he *only* has human faith in view: "Since a person is deemed right with God through faith [*pistis*] in Jesus Messiah, we also have directed faith [*pisteuo*]

toward Messiah Jesus, so that we might be deemed right by faith [*pistis*] in Messiah" (Gal. 2:16, my translation). But here is how another translation puts it: "However, we know that a person isn't made righteous by the works of the Law but rather by faith in Jesus Christ. We ourselves believed in Christ Jesus so that we could be made righteous by faith in Christ and not by works of the Law—because no one will be name righteous by the works of the Law" (CEB). Certainly Paul did not have to be concise, so this is no definitive argument that Paul had both Jesus' faith and our faith in view in this verse. But one argument for the "faithfulness" reading is how redundant the verse is otherwise.

A second argument is how similar "through the obedience of the one man the many will be made righteous" (Rom. 5:19) is to "the righteousness of God through the faithfulness of Jesus to all who have faith" (3:22, my translation)

Romans 5:19 makes it clear that Paul had a place in his thinking for the obedient, faithful death of Jesus playing a role in us becoming right with God (see also Phil. 2:6). Again, the argument is not definitive, but it once again shows that the "faithfulness" reading would fit.

Strangely enough, the passage that convinced me was 2 Corinthians 4:13: "It is written: 'I believed; therefore I have spoken.' With that same spirit of faith we also believe and therefore speak." Paul was determined to imitate that faith, so that the one who raised Jesus from the dead because of his faith (see Heb. 5:7) would raise him as well (2 Cor. 4:14). The argument is very minute, but it finally convinced me that Paul could in fact think of Jesus as having faith.

9. See especially the discussion of Galatians in the first volume in this series, *Paul—Messenger of Grace* (Indianapolis, Ind.: Wesleyan Publishing House, 2010), 133–134. In particular, one of the documents found among the Dead Sea Scrolls was called "Some of the Works of the Law" (4QMMT), and it is an argument over purity at the temple. See James VanderKam, *The Dead Sea Scrolls Today*, rev. ed. (Grand Rapids, Mich.: Eerdmans, 2010), 81–83. When Paul used this phrase in Galatians, he was especially thinking of things like circumcision that separated Jew from Gentile.

10. The collection of writings the Jews considered Scripture at this time basically consisted of three groups: (1) the Law (Torah, the first five books, the Pentateuch); (2) the Prophets (the former prophets of Joshua, Judges, Samuel, Kings, along with the latter prophets of Isaiah, Jeremiah, Ezekiel, and the twelve minor prophets); and (3) the Writings (a miscellaneous collection headed by Psalms but whose precise contents were not completely agreed on). See Luke 24:44 for a similar categorization of the Scriptures.

11. Although I cannot prove it, I wonder if the expression, "Through the faith of Jesus," was commonly known in early Christianity, perhaps even originating in Jerusalem Christianity, to where a Christian audience would immediately know it referred to Jesus' obedience to death and the atonement it entailed.

12. On the whole, I think it is more likely that the phrase "through faith" in Romans 3:25 is a reference to God's faithfulness rather than our human faith.

CHAPTER 4

1. The biblical authors did not strongly distinguish between history and the story of the Old Testament. Indeed, some Christians today, called fundamentalists, make it a key item of faith that the stories of the Bible must equate exactly with history. Dogmatism on these sorts of things has rarely made anyone godlier or resulted in greater unity or faith. Rather, it has engendered needless argument and unnecessary division. What is worse, it seems to impose foreign expectations on the biblical text that, in the end, result in far more Scripture-twisting in the name of a modern debate, rather than a stance of truly listening to what the biblical texts say.

2. Paul's thinking here is quite different from Augustine, Calvin, and Wesley, who understood depravity to mean that no one was able in his or her own power even to want to do good.

3. The later Christian concepts of the natural, moral, and political image of God in human beings have also not been marred or destroyed.

4. Augustine wrongly translated Romans 5:12 in reference to Adam, in whom all sinned. Augustine believed that we were all present in Adam when he sinned and therefore we all carry the guilt of Adam's sin. But the NIV and other translations are almost certainly correct to translate the verse to say, "In this way death came to all men, *because* all sinned" (emphasis added).

5. Notice that Paul himself interpreted Genesis differently than the impression we would get from Genesis 3 on its own. There, it seems that the default for Adam and Eve was to die from the beginning and that it was only by eating from the Tree of Life that they might live forever.

6. The 2011 revision of the NIV went back to using the word *flesh* in its translation.

7. Paul talked in Romans 7 as if the mind (and presumably spirit) was not included in this part of a person (see Rom. 7:25).

8. Later Christians would hear overtones of Christ's defeat of Satan in Genesis 3:15, although certainly the original Israelite audience would not have understood the verse this way.

9. For example, in a first-century B.C. Jewish writing called the *Life of Adam and Eve*, accessed March 8, 2011, http://www.ccel.org/c/charles/otpseudepig/adamnev.htm.

10. Satan is not mentioned in any of the books from Genesis to 2 Kings, only in the very late part of 1 Chronicles and the post-exilic Zechariah. Job's subject matter may seem very old, but I would argue that the first two chapters likely come from the period after the exile.

11. For example, it was social Darwinism that fueled William Jennings Bryan's opposition to evolution. Social Darwinism was an attitude of survival of the fittest among the elite and rich entrepreneurs that was used to justify a complete disregard for the people they employed, especially their helpless workers.

12. For example, Joel B. Green, *Body, Soul, and Human Life: The Nature of Humanity in the Bible* (Grand Rapids, Mich.: Baker Academic, 2008).

CHAPTER 5

1. Whether Paul might have considered these sins for an unbelieving Jew is a question scholars probably cannot answer, given the evidence he left.

2. Kenneth Schenck, *Paul—Messenger of Grace* (Indianapolis, Ind.: Wesleyan Publishing House, 2010), 133–134.

3. It seems very likely that Paul had Gentile believers in mind in Romans 2:15. Also, in Romans 8:4, Paul was not thinking that the righteous requirement was only literally fulfilled in Christ and then figuratively fulfilled in believers. Paul was saying that the law of the Spirit literally empowers believers to keep the heart of the Jewish Law, what he called "Christ's law" in 1 Corinthians 9:21.

4. The suggestion that Paul had Adam in mind in Romans 7:9 seems to over-read the passage. Paul was presenting a logical sequence, not an autobiographical or chronological one.

5. Paul's claim here is difficult because Jews in general did believe they could keep the law appropriately to God's expectations. Some have even accused Paul of misrepresenting or misunderstanding the law. Nevertheless, we do find this same sentiment elsewhere in the New Testament (see Acts 15:10), and Paul implied the same in Galatians 6:13.

6. From the standpoint of our understanding, it is unfortunate that Paul went on in Romans 7:25 to summarize the state of his hypothetical unbelieving Jew wanting to keep the Law: "I myself in my mind am a slave to God's law, but in the sinful nature a slave to the law of sin." Just this restatement is enough for many to ignore the victory his thoughts had just pronounced through Christ.

7. John Wesley's understanding of sin was that one can wrong others without intending to do so, and one can have an evil heart without realizing it, as has sometimes been the case with those who most preached victory over sin.

8. The biggest problem with understanding Paul here is that he used the word *law* to refer to both. What we call the moral law was not a category Jews used. It was a later Christian way of processing what parts of the Old Testament Law we still keep and the parts we do not.

CHAPTER 6

1. Let me be very clear here: what the predestinarian is suggesting goes well beyond the outrage we would feel toward someone who took a newborn, tossed it in a trash bin, and left it for dead. The double predestinarian is suggesting that God makes certain people fail and then torches them in all eternity because they failed.

2. Frederick Nietzsche, "On the Genealogy of Morals" in *The Birth of Tragedy and the Genealogy of Morals*, trans. Francis Golffing (New York: Doubleday, 1956), 209.

3. Rick Warren, *The Purpose Driven Life: What on Earth am I Here For?* (Grand Rapids, Mich.: Zondervan, 2003).

4. It is true that, just as in Romans 9, Paul was not specifically talking about individuals in Romans 11. He was talking about the direction of Israel as a whole. Someone might suggest, then, that while the direction of Israel as a whole could change, Paul thought God's plan for specific individuals must remain the same. But can you see how far removed this entire discussion is from what Paul was actually talking about? Romans 9–11 is not focused on individuals but on the fate of Israel.

5. Interestingly, Paul seemed to have modified the Old Testament quotation slightly, something New Testament authors regularly felt free to do. The Greek text Paul was reading said, "The redeemer will come because of Zion." Paul—or the tradition he was using—changed it to, "The redeemer will come out of Zion."

6. This interpretation originated with John Darby in the 1800s but was popularized again by Hal Lindsey, *The Late Great Planet Earth* (Grand Rapids, Mich.: Zondervan, 1970), and Tim LaHaye and Jerry Jenkins, *Left Behind* series (Wheaton, Ill.: Tyndale, 1995).

7. The word *all* should not be taken too rigidly. The contrast in this passage is between part and whole and is general in nature. The point is not that every single Israelite would turn out to be saved.

8. This does not violate God's foreknowledge, for presumably God knew that the Ninevites would repent if he sent Jonah to them. God's

knowledge of the future not only includes what will happen if he does not intervene, but also what will happen if he does.

9. The most natural way to take the Hebrew of this verse is in relation to something that has already happened. This fuller meaning to Old Testament passages is typical of New Testament interpretation.

CHAPTER 7

1. To be clear, I am using the word *literally* in its official rather than popular sense. People often use the word *literal* to say that something really is true, as in "He literally went through the roof." But properly speaking, if someone literally went through a roof, it would mean he broke through the roof with his body.

2. The parallelism of 10:3 pushes us to take the phrase, "the righteousness of God" (KJV), in reference to human righteousness more than God's righteousness as in 1:17. Of course Paul may have intended a double entendre here and in Romans 3:21. Some like N. T. Wright insist that Paul *always* meant God's righteousness when he used the phrase (*What Saint Paul Really Said: Was Paul of Tarsus the Real Founder of Christianity?* [Grand Rapids, Mich.: Eerdmans, 1997], 103), but this approach seems excessively rigid. Wright and others are correct that the background of the phrase pushes us toward God's righteousness as the default. But ultimately the immediate literary context must cast the deciding vote.

3. Second Corinthians 5:21 sounds like a transference of sin from us to Christ: "God made him who had no sin to be sin for us, so that in him we might become the righteousness of God." And perhaps Paul did have some sort of exchange as a second meaning to this verse. But despite how intuitive this interpretation may seem, it is not the most likely first meaning of 2 Corinthians 5:21 (Kenneth Schenck, *Paul—Messenger of Grace* [Indianapolis, Ind.: Wesleyan Publishing House, 2010], 163). The phrase, "the righteousness of God," most likely refers in the first place to God's propensity to save his people and the world. Indeed, this is exactly what the immediate context of 2 Corinthians 5:11–20 is about, God's actions to save the world. And to say that Jesus became sin would perhaps invoke the idea of a sin offering, of a sacrifice, rather than Jesus transferring our sin to him or taking our punishment.

4. C. S. Lewis, *The Lion, the Witch, and the Wardrobe* (New York: MacMillan, 1970), 138–140.

5. Championed especially by Gustaf Aulén, *Christus Victor: An Historical Study of the Three Main Types of the Idea of Atonement* (London, Society for Promoting Christianity, 1950).

6. Although most translations render Galatians 2:20, "I live by faith in the Son of God," it might just as well be translated, "I live in the faithfulness of the Son of God."

7. If Paul's understanding developed in 2 Corinthians 5:1–10, this could also refer to what happens to us at death.

CHAPTER 8

1. For explanation, see Jostein Gaarder, *Sophie's World: A Novel About the History of Philosophy*, trans. Paulette Moller (New York: Berkley, 1991), 69–71.

2. In that sense, spiritual gift tests often seem to miss the point, which was not to provide pigeonholes into which we should place ourselves.

3. This is possible, especially if Romans 16 gives greetings to individuals at Rome. However, I also argue that it is more likely the chapter was directed to the churches at Ephesus.

4. See Kenneth Schenck, "Disagreement and Disorder at Corinth," in *Paul—Messenger of Grace* (Indianapolis, Ind.: Wesleyan Publishing House, 2010), 98–121.

5. The entire burnt offering of Jewish culture was unique to Israel.

6. John Wesley described it as a "voluntary transgression of a known law [of God]," in "On Perfection," *The Works of John Wesley*, 3rd ed., vol. VI (Kansas City, Mo.: Beacon Hill, 1979), 417.

CHAPTER 9

1. At this time, Nero had not yet turned out to be the nefarious emperor we think him to be, but certainly Paul would have had no illusions about the vice that permeated the Roman system.

2. For this reason, we have to take great care when applying 1 Peter to today's society. It was not written for a situation where one might attempt to transform the very structures of society. In that respect, it would be sub-Christian to settle in our day and age for the status quo of 1 Peter. God wants to do much more in our world!

3. Acts may want us to hear an echo in Peter's statement of what Socrates said when he was on trial; Plato, *Apology*, 29d.

4. James Dobson, *Love Must Be Tough: New Hope for Families in Crisis* (Dallas: Word Books, 1983).

5. Psalm 72 was a key text in a presentation by David Gushee, "Scripture, Government and the World's Poor" (lecture, Wheaton College, Wheaton, Ill., May 18, 2010).

6. This fact does not, however, settle the issue for us today. In a situation where we can affect law, the question is whether a society moves closer to the kingdom by not having capital punishment, an issue that is currently a matter of debate among Christians.

CHAPTER 10

1. One of the books mentioned in *Paul—Messenger of Grace* to mastering Paul's writings is Wayne A. Meeks, *The First Urban Christians: The Social World of the Apostle Paul* (New Haven, Conn.: Yale University Press, 1983). It masterfully analyzes passages like Romans 16.

2. Prophets were not writers; they were speakers. We should picture the prophets speaking their prophecies in context, probably in a much different order than they currently appear in our Bibles. In the case of Isaiah, chapters 36–39 do not even claim to come from Isaiah; they are taken word for word from 2 Kings. The last twenty-seven chapters assume a situation some two hundred years after Isaiah and talk about events from that time as if they were currently happening.

3. See E. Randolph Richards, *Paul and First-Century Letter Writing: Secretaries, Composition and Collection* (Downers Grove, Ill.: IVP Academic, 2004).

4. Interestingly, the seven individuals appointed seem rather to have embarked on a prophetic ministry (see Acts 21:8). The problem at Jerusalem seems to have been much deeper than simply waiting tables. There was likely a cultural problem in which an important segment of the Greek-speaking community—was not being ministered to because Peter and the others were from a different language and culture.

5. See Kenneth Schenck, "Disagreement and Disorder," in *Paul—Messenger of Grace* (Indianapolis, Ind.: Wesleyan Publishing House, 2010), 109–113.

6. Ibid., 33–36.

7. One such copy is the New Testament papyrus known as p46. This manuscript goes on, however, to include chapter 16.

8. The first time we know of someone even suggesting the exact list of books we now have in our New Testament was in an Easter letter by an early Christian named Athanasius in the year A.D. 367. By about A.D. 400, Christians seem to have been in general agreement. By this time, the doxology of Romans had apparently been well-established for over two centuries.

9. One may sense the implications of my line of thinking here. It is to come full circle on the kinds of issues over which some previous generations vigorously fought. Most Bibles have left the endings of Mark and

Romans and the story of the woman caught in adultery (John 8) in the main text of the Bible, even while notifying the reader that it is not likely they were original. They have done so because these texts have played an important role in the history of Christianity. If the goal is not necessarily to determine the original reading, then we can see that the textual tradition behind the King James Version may not have been original, but God did just fine with it in the church for some sixteen hundred years. I am not arguing that we return to it, only that it was just as legitimately the church's text of the Bible as any modern version with the antiquarian aim of rendering the exact original.

Apply Paul's Teaching to Everyday Life

Soldier of Peace Bible Studies

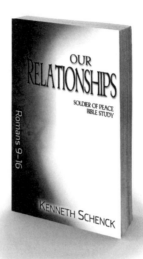

The life and writings of Paul make up a large percentage of the New Testament. Yet many Christians struggle to grasp their significance because the culture and concerns they address seem so far removed from our own life experience. The Soldier of Peace Bible Study series, based on Kenneth Schenck's *Paul— Soldier of Peace*, helps small groups and individuals go deeper in their understanding of Paul and his letters.

Like the book, these studies begin with sound scholarship and focus on applying Paul's life and letters to contemporary life in a practical way.

Each six-week study focuses on one of Paul's letters from the later part of his ministry and includes both weekly and daily study components.

Our Righteousness
Romans 1–8
$7.99
ISBN 9780898274431

Our Relationships
Romans 9–16
$7.99
ISBN 9780898274448

wesleyan
publishing
house

www.wesleyan.org/wph or call toll free
1.800.493.7539 M–F 8 a.m.–4:30 p.m. ET

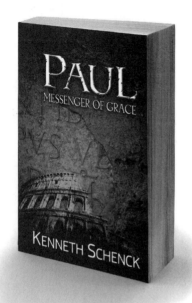
  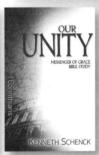 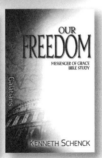